Suited for the Call

Help for the Helpmeet

Thaddette M. Smith

Forward

ೖ\ೂ

During the course of an individual's life, they are, at times, granted with the rare privilege of living in a generation when great discoveries are made. If fortunate, some of these individuals may not only witness history from afar, but also be presented with the unique opportunity to be a part of the moment. These life-changing moments possess the energy to transform cultures, lifestyles and mindsets forever. It is these extraordinary events that stamp into time a permanent impression of the hope, life, and excitement that it creates. Whether it's a new emerging technology, a life-alternating invention or life-saving medical breakthrough, man's innate ability to unleash creative power to research and diligently pursue to discover, has been rewarded with the zephyr breeze of Heaven's approval; thereby placing them in a moment of unveiled secrets. Likewise, *"Suited for the Call"*, places us at the nucleus of one of those extraordinary moments. The insight, wisdom and practical candor this book conveys is sure to change the life of every reader forever. Every woman, married or single, will forever be enlightened and strengthen. You will discover, that you are not alone in life's pursuits, challenges and experiences; but, find that there is help specifically tailored for you.

King Solomon, one of Israel's most famous kings, was notably the wisest man who every lived, spoke this great proverb. *"House and riches are an inheritance from "earthly" fathers, but a prudent wife is from the Lord."* (Proverb 19:14). This wise man articulates that man has the ability to make sound investment decisions to create generational wealth, but with all his knowledge, business savvy and experience, apart from God, his attempt to choose one of life's most precious treasures, the suitable wife, would be futile. He emphasizes that only the Heavenly Father can choose the suitable women for a man. Similarly, it is only the Heavenly Father who truly knows what the *suitable* woman needs to maximize her full potential and unveil the true essence of her beauty. Thus, God has opened through this writing, the beginning of a whole new world of revelation, healing, development, and long sought answers, that every woman can use to become the God given help-meet He has created her be: the crescendo of His creation. Therefore, take the journey with Shelly and know that you are truly suited. I promise you will never be the same again.

As Shelly's husband and certainly, best friend, I am so proud and amazed by the insight she reveals. Sweetheart, you are truly a virtuous woman; a priceless treasure who has masterfully been placed in this moment in time to help bring healing, freedom and newness of life to every reader. Bravo!

Contents

◑◐

The day of the martyr has passed. The truth is, you can't give anything you have not first received. Get what you need from God first, so He can use you to give to others. An empty vase, no matter how beautiful, cannot pour out!

Get ready. Get set. Go! All excuses must be dealt with here. All lies of the enemy, present or past, must be squashed. God created you specifically for His purpose, so ask yourself, "How can I not have all I need?" The truth must be told because it is time to go!

We must have spent our time with God first. Just as Eve was brought by God to Adam, we must also have spent time with Him alone so He can make us into what He would have us to be.

Just as Sarai was chosen to birth the *"son of the promise"* (Gen. 17:16), we too have been chosen by God for a purpose. Even as the Lord chose Rebekah for Isaac (Gen. 24:14), He also has chosen us. We must be prepared and willing to go.

We must first recognize our callings and then, just as important, recognize what we are not called to do. Then we can operate under the power of God with His direction to fulfill our purposes while keeping harmony in our homes.

"Helping" him can actually hurt you. Make sure your choices to please your husband also please God. Sometimes what appears to be good may not be godly, and what appears to be pleasing to our senses is not always what is pleasing to God. We must examine everything we give our husbands.

Now that we know what we can give him, God helps us give it to him right. The approach and our attitude to a solution are sometimes more important than the solution. In giving anyone an answer, we must make sure we give it right.

God gave us a lesson in Ephesians to help us know our time in Him. The days of Wonder Woman have long passed away; we should not try to do everything. God has our lives in seasons, and although we cannot do everything now, in His timing and in His purpose God will bring everything He has for us to pass.

God took the woman from the side of the man, from his rib. It is awesome how God chose a natural member of the body, the rib, to mimic the spiritual role of the woman. Let's see together just how the woman's role in protecting her husband's anointing is just like the rib's role in protecting the body.

Introduction

And the Reason Is . . .
ରୀ(ଙ

Helpmeet (Hebrew, ezer ke-negdo):"a help, as his counterpart," "a suitable help to him," "a wife"; "a helper suitable for or complementing him"

Genesis 2:18: *"And the LORD God said, It is not good that the man should be alone; I will make him an help meet for him."*

As I was inspired to write this book, I did not believe its main purpose was to help marriages, although it may. It was not written to strengthen the bonds between husbands and wives, although it may cause closer relationships. Nor was it written to side with one gender and tell the other it is doing things all wrong. I am not trying to name or classify anyone's call, role, or position. Nor am I trying to rate a particular anointing or office as higher or more important than another. The truth about each of us is found in the Word of God. *"For as we have many members in one body, and all members have not the same office"* (Rom. 12:4).

The fact of the matter is, each of us is equally important in our assigned capacities. Therefore, it would be wrong for me to try to put a limitation on God's creation and say the only role for a woman, for example, is to be a wife, because that is not true. The only reason, I am putting these words onto paper is to help the anointed helpmeet.

In today's times, the helpmeet has been pulled out of the traditional, safe place of tranquility in the garden of Eden and pushed into a world where she is expected to be not only wife and mother, but also stepmother, employer, employee, grandmother, aunt, sister, daughter, daughter-in-law, friend, and so much more. She is expected to be supportive, encouraging, consoling, nurturing, and encouraging, while at the same time maintaining beauty and sophistication. Since we have gone this far, let's just pull out the whole list. What about the expectation for her to cook, clean, tutor, uplift, cheer on, shield, and create a home of peace where her family may come to feel safe and loved? Again, I have put these words onto paper to help the anointed helpmeet.

And while doing all this, she must and needs to maintain an intimate relationship with her Lord and Savior, Jesus Christ, always seeking Him for direction, knowing she needs God's love and peace working constantly in her and through her life. Her relationship with God through Jesus Christ must be maintained because at any time she may be called on to help.

But without God being her life support, she will not be of any help. If her husband is hurting and being beaten by the world, she can do nothing unless God anoints her words and hands to comfort and encourage him. If her children are hurting and sick, it is only God, after she has given them all of man's medicine, who must ultimately heal them. When family and friends call, especially those not walking with the Lord, she wants to always be in a posture to show them the God in her life so they can be led to God through Christ Jesus. Thus these words have been put onto paper to help the anointed helpmeet.

To think of the number of lives she may be called on to touch in just a week, or even in a day, could be over-whelming when you consider it all. So I am putting these words onto paper to encourage her that she can do all these things and more with the grace of God. God's Word confirms in Philippians 4:13 that she *"can do all things through Christ which strengtheneth him"(her).*

Therefore, my main purpose is to encourage and strengthen all the anointed, beautiful, God-suited, fearfully-and-wonderfully-made helpmeets around the world, regardless of their present conditions or situations. There is help for them, especially those women who walk closely with their anointed husbands, not to tell them what to do, but rather to give them encouragement in what they are already doing! Finally, I must say I am putting these words to paper to help the anointed helpmeet.

A Note to the Girls

Okay, ladies, before we get started, I have to come clean with you, since we are going to be sharing a lot in the next few pages. The truth is, I have made some of my biggest mistakes, blunders, screwups— whatever you want to call them, in my marriage. I am guilty of saying and doing things that I know have hurt and even sometimes hindered my husband. I can't even say there has never been an argument between my husband and me. So I am not writing this book because I feel like I have arrived or because I have all the answers. The opposite is more the truth!

To be totally honest, sometimes it seems as if staying married is one of the hardest things I have had to do. Today's society tells us not to fight for our marriages, but to quit as soon as we have to work for or at something. In this case, our marriages, we are told, "You should not go through that," or "It should not be this hard."

Unfortunately in our society, we are told to give up on something we must work for. This microwave society tells us to expect everything in sixty seconds or less. And we should always want younger, newer, faster, or bigger. But in all these cases, what we're getting may not be better. So ladies, I had to learn to stick with it and die to my flesh and persevere. And the only thing I can say is, "But for the grace of God."

When God told me to write this book, I was in what I thought was one of the lowest times in my life. I could not imagine I would have anything worthwhile to say, let alone give a word that could encourage and speak life to the women of God. But girls, it was in my times of needing encouragement that God told me to encourage. It was when I as the helpmeet called out to Him to please send me some help that He did. Quite honestly, this book is healing and ministering to me even as I write the words. So I pray it also blesses you.

I pray in reading this book that you find how valuable you are as a wife in the kingdom of God, how special you are in the sight of God, and that you then find renewed joy in one of your many purposes in God: that of a suitable helpmeet. I pray these words excite and give you renewed strength, causing you to seek God for new understanding of what He wants to give you, not just what you are to give.

So ladies, let's begin our search and explore God's Word. Let's read it, ingest it, and allow it to renew our minds and encourage our souls. Let's seek Him together until He reveals His truth to us, making us free. Let's examine our lives, not by one another's standards, but by the standard of God's Word. The awesome thing is, even as I am writing, I am taking this journey with you ladies, my sisters.

So, let's pray and let's go!

Prayer for Our Journey

Heavenly Father, we thank You for the loving
Father that You are.
You are always caring for us and desiring for us to
become more.
Thank You, God, for supplying all our needs
and for equipping us with purpose and with all the
gifts we need to accomplish Your will.
Thank You, God, for giving each of us a measure of
faith to please You,
because without faith we cannot please You.
Thank You, God, for loving us so much that You
gave us Your Holy Word
whereby we can study and find ourselves in it,
allowing your Word to develop us
into seasoned women of God.
Thank You for providing a place in your Holy Word
where we can find every answer to our questions
and find our healing, find our deliverance, and find
our encouragement.
Thank You, God, for what You are going to do in
us as we seek after You and read this book.
Help us, God, to retain only the revealed truth.
Help us, God, to hear only Your voice.
Help us, God, to find our purpose and then delight
in that purpose,
fully embracing Your will for our lives.
And God, help to renew our minds to let go of old
traditional thoughts,
and revive our spirits so that we can do Your will
with new strength.
God, for all that You do with, for, and through us,
we will give You all the glory, praise, and honor.

Now God, as we read, have Your way.
We pray You will minister to us through Your Word
so we will always remain in Your perfect will.
In the name of our Lord, Jesus Christ, we pray.
Amen.

Chapter 1

Help Yourself First!
〰

Become, Go, and Do!

Romans 8:29–30: *"For whom he did foreknow, he also did predestinate to be conformed to the image of his Son, that he might be the firstborn among many brethren. Moreover whom he did predestinate, them he also called: and whom he called, them he also justified: and whom he justified, them he also glorified."*

I cannot stress this truth enough: the most important relationship in our lives is our relationship with God through Jesus Christ. In all we are called to do and everywhere we are called to go, we must take God or, shall I say, God must take us. It is impossible to fulfill His purpose in our lives without Him, because how will we know where to go or what to say unless He first tells us? How will we get direction unless He first gives guidance? I know as women we are gifted by God in many situations to think fast on our feet, to handle the largest to the smallest details. To work or think about multiple tasks is second nature. We have mastered multitasking.

But the truth is, we still need God before we can become all He desires us to be.

I want to introduce for the purpose of our discussion a continuous three-step process I have named Become, Go, and Do: becoming what God has predestined, going where God has sent us, and effectively doing what fulfills our purpose.

Let's start with an illustration. Once when my son, who was two at the time, and I were sitting in an airplane moments before takeoff, the flight attendant began giving instructions on what to do in case we encountered an emergency situation during the flight. One of her instructions was the use of the oxygen masks. She said if the aircraft was to lose cabin pressure, the masks would be released and drop down in front of us. She explained how to pull the masks down and forward to begin the oxygen flow.

These instructions were quite simple and easy to follow until she said, "If you are traveling with a small child, put the mask on yourself first, make sure you get sufficient oxygen, and then give an oxygen mask to your child." For some reason, this did not seem right to me, and I kept thinking she had to be wrong; I reasoned with myself that I should help my child first. The stewardess's statement seemed to go against everything I believed as a mother.

I kept thinking, He needs me. I need to protect and help him first. I thought to myself, God gave this child to me to watch over, protect, and shelter. Surely I could handle pressure drops and low oxygen levels in the plane far better than a child. I would not panic. I would understand what was happening. I would just put the mask on my son; then, after my son was stabilized, I would use the oxygen myself. Surely this flight attendant had made a mistake.

However, after careful thought, the illogical became logical. The airline's solution was really the only answer. If my child were given oxygen first, then I could possibly lose consciousness. If this happened, my son might not know how to put the oxygen mask on me, or he might not be able to lift me up to the mask to revive me. But on the other hand, an adult could easily lift an unconscious child to the mask. An adult with the proper training would know what to do with the oxygen mask, and even an adult without the correct training could still scream out and ask for help. But a child might not be able to do either of those things. The fact that the adult uses the mask first ensures that the adult will survive and in turn ensures the child's survival. The adult will be able to continue to monitor and even protect the child in the event of a future emergency.

The airline had the correct order; the helper must be helped first! See, ladies, your relationship with God through Christ Jesus is all about you and Him. This relationship must be first! God loves you first as His child, and He wants you to know Him and His will for your life first, thus the beginning of the three-step process of Become, Go, and Do.

First, we must become; then we go so that we can do. Sometimes we think we are an engineer, an evangelist, a preacher, nurse, doctor, lawyer, etc., but the truth of the matter is, these are only compositions, slivers of who we are or what we do. Each of us is first a spirit with a soul that lives in a body. Thus we must first allow God to satisfy our spirits and then allow Him to mature and renew our souls before we can effectively perform His will in our bodies.

Sometimes we change God's process and skip the spirit and the soul development and just expect the body to do God's perfect will. But our main purpose in life is to be like Christ, to become like Him. Romans 8:29–30 says, *"For whom he did foreknow, he also did predestinate to be conformed to the image of his Son, that he might be the firstborn among many brethren. Moreover whom he did predestinate, them he also called: and whom he called, them he also justified: and whom he justified, them he also glorified."* God is looking for sons and daughters who will be conformed to the image of His firstborn Son, living their lives after His life example, looking to the Word of God for direction, and always becoming more like Christ. This transformation is achieved by having an intimate relationship with the Father, studying the Word of God, knowing the Father's will for our lives, and letting the Word renew our minds, thus strengthening the spirit man continually.

Then, as a result of the process of becoming, justification and glorification come. You see, we need to first become sons and daughters in His image; then once we have become, we can go and effectively do.

God wants you to be loved and nurtured so you can become the you He intended. You cannot effectively seek God for someone else's needs unless you first seek Him for yourself. As you seek after God, He in turn pours into you, growing you, nurturing you, maturing you, and developing you so that you can become. One thing many of us fail to realize is that we must become before we can go or do.

Let's look at an example of a nursing mother. A mother who is nursing her child gives the child nourishment through her body. If the mother stops getting nourishment herself, her body will begin to decline or stop producing the same quantity or quality of nourishment. The mother must nourish herself first in order to continue to provide for her child.

This illustration demonstrates that you can't give what you haven't first received. In this case, the woman is nursing her child. But nursing is not who she is, it is what she does. She had to first be (become) a healthy woman before she could adequately do the nursing. Sometimes you might forget that what you do for your loved ones is not who you are. You must nourish, or help, yourself first!

You must remember that you are first the favored and chosen child of God, made for His pleasure and His purpose. You need your creator; He is the only one who knows the entirety of your purpose. He is the only one who knows the end of your story. The Word of God tells us in Jeremiah 29:11, *"For I know the thoughts that I think toward you, saith the LORD, thoughts of peace, and not of evil, to give you an expected end."*

You need an intimate relationship with God so that He can show you what to become. Your need for God is not an option, but a necessity. This is who you are, though the what-you-do could range from wife, mother, evangelist, pastor, or businesswoman to whatever God says.

As God develops you and you become, the more you can do! But don't seek God for what you are called to do; seek God to be and to become. The more He talks to you, the more He builds you, the inner man. God's Word records in Ephesians 3:16, *"That he would grant you, according to the riches of his glory, to be strengthened with might by his spirit in the inner man."* The stronger your inner man, the stronger you become and the more you can do. So stay connected to God.

John 15:4–5 says, *"Abide in me, and I in you. As the branch cannot bear fruit of itself, except it abide in the vine; no more can ye, except ye abide in me. I am the vine, ye are the branches: He that abideth in me, and I in him, the same bringeth forth much fruit: for without me ye can do nothing."* The truth in the Scriptures is that we need God for everything. We must remain connected to Him and allow Him to nourish us. God must strengthen our inner man. Only then can we effectively help others. This can be achieved in our daily time with God through prayer, meditation on His Word, and an attitude of praise.

First, the daily reading of God's Word is like being reintroduced to your best friend every day. During this time, your best friend reveals to you another aspect or dimension of Himself so you can understand Him better and each day learn something more about Him. The daily reading of God's in a later chapter, but know you are not alone, and earnestly seeking God through prayer is the key.

My prayer life has become my life strength. God has so graciously made a way for us to come to the Father boldly and let our praises and petitions be heard. Hebrew 4:16 says, "Let us therefore come boldly unto the throne of grace, that we may obtain mercy, and find grace to help in time of need." God so loves us that He wishes to commune with us, always. He loves to speak to us and hear from us. This is wonderful, because the God who created everything wants to know what we have to say. Wow!

He says to cast our cares on Him, for He cares for us. As 1 Peter 5:7 says, *"Casting all your care upon him, for he careth for you."* Isn't this spectacular? But the tragedy is having the ability to come to the Father but never taking advantage of the opportunity. I love the Scripture in Hebrews because it specifies "in time of need." When we need His grace, we will have His grace.

God says to us, "Talk to Me. I want to hear what yo have to say, because I have so much to tell you and confirm to you in prayer." There cannot be a loving and growing relation-ship without the parties communicating. See, I was saved and had given my life to the Lord, but my relationship with God was one-sided: it was centered on me. I used to talk about my problems to others or rewind the situation in my mind and think about it over and over again. In essence, I would talk to myself or others, and God could listen in. But I never really prayed about it.

Eventually I noticed this never accomplished anything except to feed my flesh. I was giving all my power to the problem by rehearsing it. It was as if I were glorifying the problem. I would find myself getting frustrated, panicked, anxious, or angry over the same things again and again.

However, one day I made a conscious decision to pray instead of talk. Even the times when I did not know what to pray, I would just pray for God's will to be done in my life. As I prayed and sought the Lord, He began to show me His will through His Word. I began to build my spirit man instead of my flesh. Now I would think about a God who could solve any problem.

You must turn the tables and glorify God, and He will solve all your problems. Find a definite refuge in Him through prayer.

The last area we need to discuss is my favorite: praise. Praise is the icing on the cake. There have been times in my life that I felt so heavy and when it seemed as if I could not read the Word to receive or focus in prayer. But I would just begin to thank God for just being God, not for fixing anything, but just for being God. I would start exalting the name of the Lord, praising Him for being wonderful, great, mighty, good, omnipotent, faithful, and holy. These words would elevate my spirit.

I know sometimes this is difficult, but don't give up; stay persistent. Proclaim Him Lord and Savior in every area and situation in your life. Sometimes I would just say hallelujah until I knew something broke in the spirit and the spirit of heaviness was gone.

You know, the best part of praise is that it often turns into worship. As you worship God and enter into His presence, He may not change your situation, but He is ministering and changing you. You cannot go into the presence of God and return the same. So I encourage you, sisters, praise God until your praise takes you into His presence. The enemy can't keep you down when you enter into His presence. You have a right, as a matter of a fact, it is a command, just because you have breath in your body; read Psalm 150:6. Praise is a state of mind. You can praise God anywhere and anytime. Never let opportunities to praise God pass you by!

Daily prayer, reading God's Word, and praising His name will work together to renew your mind, encourage your soul, and revive your spirit. And then the joy of the Lord can truly be your strength. As Nehemiah 8:10 says, *"Neither be ye sorry; for the joy of the LORD is your strength."*

We have discussed a lot in this first chapter, but I want to stress again that you must first have your own relationship with God so He can continually pour into you. Be careful not to sell yourself short! You need all the time you can get with God, and the more time you spend with Him in His Word, in prayer, and in singing His praises, the stronger you will become and the more you will intimately know Him. So let Him pour into you first, and then you can pour Him out to others!

I want to end this chapter with one more illustration. You may have heard of Waterford crystal. A Waterford vase is considered valuable to the creator and often to the individual who has purchased or been given one. But the beauty of the vase is useless to the creator or the redeemer if he or she cannot use the vase to pour into and subsequently pour out of. You see, in that case the vase is not being used for what it was created. I am sure the creator wanted the outward beauty to be noticed. But the purpose was for the vase to be poured into and then used.

I believe we are sometimes just like that Waterford vase. You see, our creator wants to pour into us so we can be used. We are valuable because of the time He has taken to mold us, to blow into us and shape us into the beautiful vessels we are. But to never be able to use us would be a waste. Don't let your purpose be wasted. Let Him pour in so you can pou out.

Chapter 1

Help Yourself First!

Chapter Prayer

God, thank You for caring for me and loving me.
I thank You for the ability to know You for myself and
not just through others.
God, thank You for calling me unto You,
just as I am, with all my flaws and inadequacies.

Thank You, God, for sending Your Son, Jesus,
that I might be redeemed and adopted into the body
of Christ.

God, I now recommit myself to Your Word and to prayer
so You can continue to unveil Yourself to me and
increase my inner man.
Teach me, Lord, to depend on You.
Show me Your will, purpose, and destiny for my life.

And in the name of Jesus,
I bind every hindering spirit and demonic force
that would try to come against my relationship with You,
every plan, plot, or attack that would attempt to separate
me from You.
I curse it in the name of Jesus, and it will not prosper.

God, help me to be the person You desire
so I can become, go, and do Your divine will.

In the name of Jesus, I pray.
Amen.

Chapter 2

Made Suitable

๑๖

Helpmeet (Hebrew, ezer ke-negdo):"a help, as his counterpart," "a suitable help to him," "a wife"; "a helper suitable for or complementing him"

Genesis 2:18: *"And the LORD God said, It is not good that the man should be alone; I will make him an help meet for him"*.

The second chapter of Genesis is such a rich text for revealing some of the thoughts of the Creator where women are concerned. As we begin to understand more about the term helpmeet, let us look to God for definition and understanding of what He has called (made) us to be.

Concerning the creation of man and woman, the Bible says in Genesis 1:27, *"God created man in his own image, in the image of God created he him; male and female created he them."* Genesis 2:18 continues with, *"And the LORD God said, It is not good that the man should be alone; I will make him an help meet for him."* Genesis 2:21–22 adds: *"And the LORD God caused a deep sleep to fall upon Adam, and he slept: and he took one of his ribs, and closed up the flesh instead thereof; And the rib, which the LORD God had taken from man, made he a woman, and brought her unto the man."*

We already know from Genesis 1:27 that the woman was created in the image of God, but the full explanation of her creation is explained in the second chapter of Genesis, verses 4 through 25. As we read the text, we see Gods creation.

Lets look at God creation, the bible records, in the beginning God created the heavens and the earth. The earth until now was formless and empty. God separated the light from the darkness, he separated the water under the expanse from the water above it and called the expanse "sky." God caused the water under the sky be gathered to one place, and let dry ground appear; calling the dry ground "land," and the gathered waters he called "seas." Then God commanded the land to produce vegetation: seed-bearing plants and trees on the land that bear fruit with seed in it, according to their various kinds. God created the lights in the expanse of the sky to separate the day from the night, and mark the seasons and days and years. God made two great lights, the greater light to govern the day and the lesser light to govern the night. He also made the stars. Now, God created the great creatures of the sea and every living and moving thing with which the water teems, according to their kinds, and every winged bird according to its kind. God made the wild animals according to their kinds, the livestock according to their kinds, and all the creatures that move along the ground according to their kinds. Then God said, "Let us make man in our image, in our likeness, and let them rule over the fish of the sea and the birds of the air, over the livestock, over all the earth, and over all the creatures that move along the ground."

Then the Lord God formed man of the dust of the ground and breathed into his nostrils the breath of life, and man became a living soul. After all this, it would seem that the garden was complete. But God in His omniscience knew there was one more creation to be brought forth. So God began Eve's coming forth by announcing a situation or what looked to be an area of need for Adam. *"It is not good that the man should be alone,"* says Genesis 2:18. Also, recorded in verse 20, Scripture says, *"But for Adam there was not found an help meet for him."* Isn't God awesome? He announced something "not good" so He could create a "good thing." Thank You, Jesus! As Proverbs 18:22 says, *"Whosoever findeth a wife findeth a good thing, and obtaineth favour of the LORD."*

One thing that stands out to me in reading Genesis 1 and 2 is that God identified the condition, or need, of Adam, and then He spoke the answer. The fact that God was going to answer Adam's need was done without Adam's help or involvement. God never asked Adam anything; there was no meeting or conference. God's answer was to handle everything alone. In fact, He took Adam out! *"He caused a deep sleep to fall upon Adam"* (Gen. 2:21).

And just as God didn't need Adam's help then, He doesn't need our help now! The text never records God asking Adam what he thought, wanted, or needed. The Bible does not record God asking Adam if the answer should be tall, short, big, small, soft-spoken, extremely loud, shy, outgoing, blonde, red-haired, or brunette. God never asked Adam's opinion.

Can you image what that conversation would have been like? "So Adam, how should she be formed? Which areas should be curved, rounded, soft?" Or "Adam, what should her interests be? What should her likes or dislikes be?" Nothing like this is ever recorded!

The next thing we read is that God made woman and said she was "good," as in Proverbs 18:22. God completely fulfilled Adam's need without recorded input from Adam. But look at the awesomeness of God: God answered a need in Adam's life without Adam even knowing he was lacking. And He answered it completely. After God made Eve, the

Bible does not record God creating anything else. Eve was the answer, a complete gift, a woman.

The key point is God alone knew Adam's need completely, and God alone answered the need completely. He made the woman suitable to meet the need. To say that God would identify a need in our lives and fill that need incompletely would be like saying that God did not have enough foresight to adequately provide for us. We know this is impossible, because God is sovereign; He knows all and can do all. He knew Adam's need, and He made a woman who was totally equipped with gifts, talents, and abilities to meet the need. God knows His will for our lives and futures, the people we are to meet and the places we must go. He equips us even before we know we have a need in our lives.

I must pause here to make sure we are all still together. I don't mean to imply that a woman's sole purpose is to be born and raised only to meet her husband, marry him, and live the rest of her life in his shadow. I personally think the contrary is the truth. But I do want to help the women of God who are married and may sometimes feel overwhelmed or incapable of meeting all of life's challenges as a wife. I want to encourage them that God has completely equipped them, and they are made suitable.

Although God has many purposes for us as wives, we must never forget He has made us suitable for this purpose. Remember the Waterford vase: the creator knew the purpose before he began the creation. The making was with purpose in mind. Every step of the process was performed so the vase would be prepared for its purpose. The process ensures, of course, that the vase is suitable for use.

As a suitable helpmeet, you need to recognize God has already made you wonderful. He has already equipped you to be the helpmeet. He spoke your role into existence, and then He created you to fulfill what He spoke. Since God's Word cannot return to Him void, then you must be what He called you. Remember His word in Isaiah 55:11; it says, *"So shall My word be that goeth forth out of my mouth: it shall not return unto me void, but it shall accomplish that which I please, and it shall prosper in the thing whereto I sent it."* So, women of God, do not be intimidated; do not let your past hinder you. Put your focus on your creator and what He called you to be. Accept what God has spoken about your life, and walk in the gifts He has equipped you with. You are suited for the call.

Once when I was feeling inadequate, God gave me reassurance through this illustration: When a female child is born, her body naturally has everything she needs, meaning her body either has it or is capable of producing it. For example, a female child already has or will produce all the reproductive eggs she needs for the remainder of her life. As her body begins to change and she matures into womanhood, her body begins to produce eggs on a monthly cycle. A female child already has on the inside what the adult woman needs. The process of growth and maturity is what brings forth the ability to meet the purpose.

Therefore, God has given you as part of the provision for His "pre-vision." What do I mean by "pre-vision"? It is what God has purposed and fore seen you would become, go and do. Remember, all that you need to be suitable has already been supplied by the Father. If your husband is a visionary and he can see from A to Z but maybe does not know how to go from A to B, then ask God to help you with the details. Then, as your husband speaks vision, you can help him write it and make it plain so that he who reads it can run with it. You might even be the one running! Or it could be that your husband is a gifted businessman; he may be gifted to negotiate large deals, but the day-to-day operation of balancing the checkbook might get away from him from time to time. Again, ask God to show you the way to help. Maybe you are more equipped to handle that area in your home.

So stay encouraged, even when people say you don't look like his wife, or begin to tell you all the things that are wrong with you, or even when you doubt yourself and the enemy tries to speak to your insecurities, causing you to second guess yourself and not step out into your purpose. Please remember, it is in your weakness that God shows Himself strong. Feelings of weakness or incapability of doing all that God has asked you to do can be answered in God's Word. As 2 Corinthians 12:9 says, *"And he said unto me, My grace is sufficient for thee: for my strength is made perfect in weakness."* We are not perfect; we do have shortcomings, and there will be times we don't do things right. But we must continually seek the Lord. Remember, even in your mistakes, there is no condemnation in Christ Jesus. Ask God to forgive you, thank Him for understanding, and press on. Let Him continually make you until you become what He has purposed for you in your marriage. Seek God first and ask Him what you should change and what you should leave. Ask God to change you for His purpose, not for anyone else's. Remember, God is your creator and author, so go to Him for every question or doubt you have concerning yourself or your future. God is the only one who really knows what areas need to be changed in your life. Let His Word wash you and make you new.

Again God's Word gives us confirmation. Jeremiah 29:11 says, *"For I know the thoughts that I think toward you, saith the* Lord, *thoughts of peace, and not of evil, to give you an expected end."* You see, God has always known what His plans were for your life. Included in your life is your marriage, so let God change you. He is your author and creator; He is the only one who can make you into who you need to be, so let Him continue.

You are a gift from God. As a matter of fact, a gift was being made for Adam while he slept, a gift to meet all the needs God had foreseen. The only thing Adam needed to do was receive the gift. So sisters, realize you were made a suitable helpmeet, spoken into existence by God. Everything God spoke about you will come to pass because the God we know cannot lie. As Numbers 23:19 says, *"God is not a man, that he should lie, neither the son of man, that he should repent: hath he said, and shall he not do it? Or hath he spoken, and shall he not make it good? "* Therefore, walk from this day forward in that anointing, the anointing of a suitable helper!

Chapter 2

Made Suitable

Chapter Prayer

Thank You, God, for Your Word concerning me.
Thank You, God, for making me with purpose in
mind and making me suited for my purpose.
Thank You for showing me in Your Word that I
am made suitable and that You spoke over my life
before the beginning of time.

I acknowledge that everything I need, You have so
graciously given me. Lord, I thank You!
God, thank You for reminding me that You said,
"It is not good for man to be alone."
And then you called me out—
a suitable helpmeet.

God, I thank You!

Lord, I pray for the seed of Your Word concerning
me to be planted in my spirit today so that the Word
may take hold and grow and strengthen me to know
I have been made by You to be suitable for whatever
the situation.

And God, shut up every voice that would come
against my purpose.
Shut up every voice that says, "You can't do
it; every voice that says, "You don't have the
education"; every voice that says, "You don't have

the finances"; and every voice that says, "You are
not suitable for your husband."

I accept and walk from this day forward in the
anointing of being a helpmeet made suitable
by You.
In the name of Jesus,
Amen.

Chapter 3

Brought By God

ରା(ୱ

Genesis 2:22: *"And the rib, which the Lord God had
taken from man, made he a woman. And brought
her unto the man".*

The Lord God brought her unto the man. We could say
it appears that God spent more time alone with Adam
and less with Eve. It appears in Genesis 2:22 that He merely
made Eve and gave her to Adam with no thought. But as I
read this text, I am encouraged to see something different.
Genesis 2:22 says, *"And the rib, which the Lord God had
taken from man, made he a woman. And brought her unto
the man".*

As we have already said, when the time came for God to
bring Eve forth, He caused Adam to sleep. God's full inten-
tion for inoculating Adam we do not know. But we do know
that during that time, God was alone with Eve. God in His
omniscience purposed to be alone with her. While alone, just
God and the woman—He molded, created, and shaped her
life. He created her so that no one else could claim having a
hand in it. No one could say she would be this or she would
be that, or she would do this or she would do that. God alone
made her. I love it, because this was a hands-on job.

But the important thing I want you to see is that the Bible says He "brought her." For years I just read over that Scripture quickly, never giving it a second thought, until one day God showed me this: God could have brought Eve forth without the man being asleep. He did not have to be alone with her. We know He was alone with Eve because the Bible says in Genesis 2:21, *"And the Lord God caused a deep sleep to fall upon Adam, and he slept."* The Bible continues in verse 22 to say that *"...made he a woman. And brought her unto the man."* He brought her; if God and Eve were standing with Adam, why would God have to bring her to him? She didn't find Adam herself, nor did Adam walk up to Eve and find her by some accident, but God brought her to the man in His time.

This encourages me because even before God joins us to our husbands as suitable helpers, we need to have time alone with Him to get to know Him and ourselves. He wants us to be intimate with Him, not just have a relationship with Him through our husbands or someone else. God does not want us to piggyback off someone else's intimacy with Him. We must get to know Him ourselves. We must know and apprehend Him. Philippians 3:12 says, *"Not as though I had already attained, either were already perfect: but I follow after, if that I may apprehend that for which also I am apprehended of Christ Jesus."*

As I imagine, Eve was in the garden with God, and God molded, shaped, and created her as only He could. As He created Eve, His spoken word of "suitable helper" and "help-meet" manifested itself in her. And she was equipped with all He had spoken of her. Once she had spent time with her heavenly Father and He had placed within her all she would need and become, then He brought her unto the man. It makes me think of a loving father proudly walking his daughter, whom he loves, to the man who will be her husband. Although the Bible does not say this specifically, I imagine this to be the first wedding procession, with all creation as the witnesses to what God ordained as the institution of marriage.

If I could further use my imagination, Eve had to walk with her Father first before walking with Adam. She had to walk with Him as He brought her. In the same way, we must first walk with God, our heavenly Father, before ever getting to our husbands. We must first spend time with our heavenly Father to know who He is Jehovah, Abba Father; to know who He is to us and for us; to understand who we are to Him and that His purposes are for us to become, go, and do; to know from our Father first who we are the daughters of the most high King.

We are made in His image and made to subdue and have dominion. Our Father owns the cattle on a thousand hills. He is our keeper, our source, our healer, and everything we need, our Alpha and our Omega. Our heavenly Father builds our self-esteem and character and prepares us for our purpose in Him. Then, from walking with our Father, we find out who we are: His daughters, loved, favored, and chosen. And we find out what He wants from us, the places He wants us to go, and the lives we are to touch.

Some of you have come to Christ since marriage, but this concept still applies. Through your salvation, you have been made a new creature, and in being made new, you still must spend time with God. He will prepare you even while you are with your husband.

Then, once we have spent time with God, He shows us to our husbands, the great men of God that we will walk through life with. And when we are joined, God pronounces blessing over that which he brought together, just as he blessed Adam and Eve in Genesis 1:28: *"And God blessed them, and God said unto them, Be fruitful, and multiply, and replenish the earth, and subdue it: and have dominion over the fish of the sea, and over the fowl of the air, and over every living thing that moveth upon the earth."*

You see, marriage is not something we should assume we can do because everyone else is doing it. The truth is, a God-ordained marriage between two chosen children of God who are living in the will of God has no choice but to succeed. I know in this modern time we do not believe in arranged marriages. But the truth is, our heavenly Father should arrange all our marriages. Our responsibility is to be prepared for marriage by spending time with our heavenly Father. This is so God can pronounce a Genesis 1:28 blessing over us.

Do not worry about who was created first or second; just thank God for His order and purpose. Bless God because it was He who brought woman forth in His time. I imagine that God was preparing the earth in some instances just for the arrival and presentation of the woman. He colored the sky blue for her and accented it with soft clouds; he sprinkled the heavens with small stars of twinkling light. He put birds in the sky. He created every creature to be the audience of her arrival and the witness at her wedding. God had it all planned, so stay encouraged and let Him bring you. Only God knows who you are going to become and what you are going to do, so let Him bring you. And only God can completely prepare you for your arrival, so let Him prepare everything before you and then bring you.

Chapter 3

Brought By God

Chapter Prayer

God, I thank you for making me an individual.
God thank you for teaching me, I must first have a
relationship with you.
Thank you Lord

God, my heavenly Father, I thank You for
preparing for me.
God, I thank You for wanting everything ready
for my arrival.
God, I thank You for spending time with just me.

God, I pray You teach me to take advantage of
every moment alone with You.
And in those precious moments,
help me to know You as Abba Father.

Prepare me, God, in the moments we spend alone
so that when You bring me together with my
husband, my time with You shines through my
life and marriage.

Thank You, Father.

In the name of Jesus, I pray.
Amen.

Chapter 4

Chosen for the Call
ରାଡ

Jeremiah 29:11: *"For I know the thoughts that I think toward you, saith the LORD, thoughts of peace, and not of evil, to give you an expected end."*

God is so awesome, because nothing just happens. Nothing God does is a mistake. We might be in error, but God is never wrong. Once we have established a relationship with God and know Him as our Heavenly Father, He can show us how He chose us for a purpose. As He molds us and calls us out for a purpose, we know that we are chosen.

God knows what He has planned for us long before we get the understanding. He says in Jeremiah 29:11, *"For I know the thoughts that I think toward you, saith the LORD, thoughts of peace, and not of evil, to give you an expected end."* This Scripture alone should give each of us renewed peace and an overwhelming sense of security in what God has chosen for us. An example of God's providential choosing is seen in the choosing of a wife for Isaac.

The story begins with a father's concern for his son and the heavenly Father's answer, a divine choosing. The Bible records in Genesis 24:1–4:

Abraham was old, and well stricken in age: and the LORD had blessed Abraham in all things. And Abraham said unto his eldest servant of his house, that ruled over all that he had, Put, I pray thee, thy hand under my thigh: And I will make thee swear by the LORD, the God of heaven, and the God of the earth, that thou shalt not take a wife unto my son of the daughters of the Canaanites, among whom I dwell: But thou shalt go unto my country, and to my kindred, and take a wife unto my son Isaac.

I absolutely love this story because as you will see, Isaac's wife was ultimately chosen by God. Rebekah was chosen not by the servant, nor by Abraham, nor by her husband, Isaac, but by God Himself! Again, God always gives a complete gift.

This story takes us on a journey with Abraham's trusted servant who went to find Isaac a wife. Sarah had died and Abraham was an old man. Abraham was concerned about a wife for his son; he wanted to make sure Isaac had a wife. Maybe at this time Abraham was remembering the promises of God that he would be the father of many nations. Genesis 12:2 says, *"And I will make of thee a great nation, and I will bless thee, and make thy name great; and thou shalt be a blessing."* Maybe Abraham wanted to make sure they chose the right wife, or maybe Abraham didn't want Isaac to be alone if he died. At any rate, a need was present, and the heavenly Father divinely intervened with the answer.

Abraham called his servant and made him swear to go to the land of Abraham's kinsmen and bring back a wife for Isaac. One important factor here is that Isaac would not be making the journey with the eldest servant to find his wife. Genesis 24:6 says, *"And Abraham said unto him, Beware thou that thou bring not my son thither again."* It does not even say that Isaac was involved in the conversation. Abraham must have trusted the servant, to give him this great responsibility. You see, the servant would participate in the manifestation of the promise of God.

The child of the promise had no wife and no children. How could the promise continue to the next generation? But as usual God showed up and provided. The servant began the search with prayer, which should be an example to us. Genesis 24:12 says, *"And he said, O LORD God of my master Abraham, I pray thee, send me good speed this day, and show kindness unto my master Abraham..."*. This is good, because we should always seek God first for His choice.

The story continues to unfold, as Genesis 24:13–27 records:

Behold, I stand here by the well of water; and the daughters of the men of the city come out to draw water: And let it come to pass, that the damsel to whom I shall say, Let down thy pitcher, I pray thee, that I may drink; and she shall say, Drink, and I will give thy camels drink also: let the same be she that thou hast appointed for thy servant Isaac; and thereby shall I know that thou hast showed kindness unto my master. And it came to pass, before he had done speaking, that, behold, Rebekah came out, who was born to Bethuel, son of Milcah, the wife of Nahor, Abraham's brother, with her pitcher upon her shoulder. And the damsel was very fair to look upon, a virgin, neither had any man known her: and she went down to the well, and filled her pitcher, and came up. And the servant ran to meet her, and said, Let me, I pray thee, drink a little water of thy pitcher. And she said, Drink, my lord: and she hasted, and let down her pitcher upon her hand, and gave him drink. And when she had done giving him drink, she said, I will draw water for thy camels also, until they have done drinking. And she hasted, and emptied her pitcher into the trough, and ran again unto the well to draw water, and drew for all his camels. And the man wondering at her held his peace, to wit whether the LORD had made his journey prosperous or not. And it came to pass, as the camels had done drinking, that the man took a golden earring of half a shekel weight, and two bracelets for her hands of ten shekels weight of gold; And said, Whose daughter art thou? tell me, I pray thee: is there room in thy father's house for us to lodge in? And she said unto him, I am the daughter of Bethuel the son of Milcah, which she bare unto Nahor. She said moreover unto him, We have both straw and provender enough, and room to lodge in. And the man bowed down his head, and worshipped the LORD. And he said, Blessed be the LORD God of my master Abraham, who hath not left destitute my master of his mercy and his truth: I being in the way, the LORD led me to the house of my master's brethren.

Rebekah was not chosen to be Isaac's wife for any other reason than the Lord chose her. The choosing had nothing to do with her size, success, mistakes, or failures. But it was God's will for her life. The servant had not seen her the first time he prayed, so we cannot say he chose her because of her beauty or chose her himself. Neither Isaac nor Abraham had been back to their homeland since Genesis 12:1. Even in the Scriptures we read that Isaac was not to return. Genesis 24:6 says, *"And Abraham said unto him, Beware thou that thou bring not my son thither again."* Isaac did not even make the journey, let alone make the choice. So we know he had nothing to do with the choosing of his wife. Isaac had to be told all that had happened in the choosing of his wife, so we know he was not involved. Genesis 24:66 says, *"And the servant told Isaac all things that he had done."*

The beauty of God's gift was that it was able to meet both Isaac and Rebekah's needs. The love story was complete, and the Bible says, *"Isaac was comforted and he loved her."* God's gifts are always complete. Genesis 24:67 says, *"And Isaac brought her into his mother Sarah's tent, and took Rebekah, and she became his wife; and he loved her: and Isaac was comforted."*

Another witness of God's choice of a woman is found in the story of Abram and Sarai. The account of Sarai and Abram is found in Genesis, chapters 12 through 18. God had promised Abram to make his name great, but Sarai decided in chapter 16 to help God accomplish His will. Maybe Sarai thought she was the problem, the holdup. Sarai had been chosen by God to bring forth a son, the child of the promise. God's perfect will was for the promise to come through her. God had first made the promise to Abram in Genesis 12:1–3: *"Now the LORD had said unto Abram, Get thee out of thy country, and from thy kindred, and from thy father's house, unto a land that I will show thee: And I will make of thee a great nation, and I will bless thee, and make thy name great; and thou shalt be a blessing: And I will bless them that bless thee, and curse him that curseth thee: and in thee shall all families of the earth be blessed."*

After years of waiting, Sarai decided to help God. Genesis 16:1–5 says:

> *Now Sarai Abram's wife bare him no children: and she had an handmaid, an Egyptian, whose name was Hagar. And Sarai said unto Abram, Behold now, the LORD hath restrained me from bearing: I pray thee, go in unto my maid; it may be that I may obtain children by her. And Abram hearkened to the voice of Sarai. And Sarai Abram's wife took Hagar her maid*

the Egyptian, after Abram had dwelt ten years in the land of Canaan, and gave her to her husband Abram to be his wife.

And he went in unto Hagar, and she conceived: and when she saw that she had conceived, her mistress was despised in her eyes. And Sarai said unto Abram, My wrong be upon thee: I have given my maid into thy bosom; and when she saw that she had conceived, I was despised in her eyes: the LORD judge between me and thee.

The tragedy of this story is that Sarai did not know she was the chosen vessel. She was about to bring forth greatness, but she did not even know it. The promise was coming through her, and she didn't even know it! Ladies, we need to be in tune with God so that we always know what we are chosen for. Once we know this, there is no place in our lives for jealousy, envy, or covetousness. Then we can walk in our purpose fully.

Clearly, not only was Sarai Abram's wife, but God also had other purposes for her. Unfortunately, she did not know what she had been chosen to do. Therefore, she gave up on the promise of God and gave her husband away. Although during this time it was acceptable for a man to have more than one wife, if Sarai had stood on what God had told her, there would have been no need for a Hagar. This is a wonderful lesson for us today because it causes us to look at what we are giving up or giving over. And all this stems from us not fully understanding that we are chosen.

It is imperative to pause here and do a self-examination. Sarai gave Hagar to her husband in an attempt to help God fulfill his promise to Abram. The question we must ask ourselves is, have we been giving up on something and maybe even given our husbands away? So, what have you given up?

Let's continue to read. Hagar conceived and bore a son. Genesis 16:12 says, *"And the angel of the LORD said unto her, Behold, thou art with child, and shalt bear a son, and shalt call his name Ishmael; because the LORD hath heard thy affliction. And he will be a wild man; his hand will be against every man, and every man's hand against him; and he shall dwell in the presence of all his brethren."*

Then verses 15–16 say, *"And Hagar bare Abram a son: and Abram called his son's name, which Hagar bare, Ishmael. And Abram was fourscore and six years old, when Hagar bare Ishmael to Abram."*

Although Sarai thought she was helping, she actually created more of a problem. But God was still gracious towards her. God knows that sometimes we get impatient and even take matters into our own hands. We mess everything up, involve other people, and sometimes even hurt them. But look how faithful God is! He came back to Sarai, just as He often has to come back to us, and reaffirmed her and His will in her life.

Let's read in Genesis 17:15–16: *"And God said unto Abraham, As for Sarai thy wife, thou shalt not call her name Sarai, but Sarah shall her name be. And I will bless her, and give thee a son also of her: yea, I will bless her, and she shall be a mother of nations; kings of people shall be of her."*

God continued, *"Sarah thy wife shall bear thee a son indeed; and thou shalt call his name Isaac: and I will establish my covenant with him for an everlasting covenant, and with his seed after him. And as for Ishmael, I have heard thee: Behold, I have blessed him, and will make him fruitful, and will multiply him exceedingly; twelve princes shall he beget, and I will make him a great nation. But my covenant will I establish with Isaac, which Sarah shall bear unto thee at this set time in the next year"* Genesis 17:19–21.

God chose Sarai to show His glory. Genesis 17:16–19 clearly states God's choice, but the incident with Hagar was permitted. Let us review it. Genesis 17:16–19 reads:

And I will bless her, and give thee a son also of her: yea, I will bless her, and she shall be a mother of nations; kings of people shall be of her. Then Abraham fell upon his face, and laughed, and said in his heart, Shall a child be born unto him that is an hundred years old? and shall Sarah, that is ninety years old, bear? And Abraham said unto God, O that Ishmael might live before thee! And God said, Sarah thy wife shall bear thee a son indeed; and thou shalt call his name Isaac: and I will establish my covenant with him for an everlasting covenant, and with his seed after him.

It was Sarai's choice of the flesh that God permitted to show us that only His will is perfect. In these verses, Sarai willingly gave her husband to someone else. I want to stop here to ask the question again: is there anything God has promised you that you have willingly given away to someone else? Maybe it was something God promised you and your husband together, and you have gotten discouraged. Maybe it has taken longer than you thought it should.

Okay, let me ask another question: have you given your husband to someone else? Let me make it plain. Do you feel there is something he needs done or needs to happen that you just cannot do? Maybe you have decided you are too old, too short, too tall, too skinny, too fat, not anointed enough, can't speak in front of people, can't sing in front of people, or can't pray in front of people. I could go on for pages. The question still remains: have you allowed your low self-esteem or feeling of inadequacy to push your husband to another? Have you forgotten you are chosen?

Well, I just want to give you one example. I hope this makes you cringe. Imagine your husband in your mind. He is going about his day, and God gives him a God- idea. For this illustration, we will say it is a world-changing idea for a new ministry. As he is sitting at home or on his job, wherever you imagine him to be, he is so excited because first, he knows he just heard from God, and second, because he knows this will change lives and in turn change the world.

Now imagine he reaches for the phone with this God-plan burning in his heart. He needs to tell someone who will immediately agree with what God has just given him. Now imagine that he calls the church administrator or his other prayer partner or anyone else, just not you. What if you have pushed him away from calling until he automatically calls someone else? How does that image make you feel?

I do not use this example to say we should control every idea of our husbands, but we should want to be one of those that he can confide in. Once we know his vision, we should be the one to help pray over it, help nurture it, and, if need be, help carry it in the spirit until it is time to deliver. Remember, we were not just chosen to carry natural babies.

In our lives, we must remember that God has chosen us, chosen for a purpose and a specific time. At the fullness of time, He will bring out of us what only He could place in us. So rest in the understanding that you are chosen. Don't try to go before God and plan to choose another way or another person to fulfill your purpose. I encourage you to be careful in everything you choose; you must be careful that you do not get your choices, but God's. If you get your choices, the worst thing will happen: you will get what you want but give up all God has for you. Be careful of your choices!

Please remember that after being chosen, you must be willing. Do not let the enemy trick you out of your calling or your destiny in God. He wishes to cloud situations with lies to make you doubt what God has for you, to cause you to doubt that God has called you out for a specific purpose and then to doubt He has equipped you for that purpose. But the devil is a liar! Stay focused, pray always for His direction, and be willing to answer the call.

In the case of Rebekah, what would have happened if she had not been willing to return with Abraham's servant to marry Isaac? Genesis 24:5–8 and 55–61 tells the story. First, in Genesis 24:5–8, we read, *"And the servant said unto him, Peradventure the woman will not be willing to follow me unto this land: must I needs bring thy son again unto the land from whence thou camest? . . . And if the woman will not be willing to follow thee, then thou shalt be clear from this my oath: only bring not my son thither again."* The choice would be Rebekah's.

Then, in Genesis 24:55–61, we read:

> *And her brother and her mother said, Let the damsel abide with us a few days, at the least ten; after that she shall go. And he said unto them, Hinder me not, seeing the LORD hath prospered my way; send me away that I may go to my master. And they said, We will call the damsel, and enquire at her mouth. And they called Rebekah, and said unto her, Wilt thou go with this man? And she said, I will go. And they sent away Rebekah their sister, and her nurse, and Abraham's servant, and his men. And they blessed Rebekah, and said unto her, Thou art our sister, be thou the mother of thousands of millions, and let thy seed possess the gate of those which hate them. And Rebekah arose, and her damsels, and they rode upon the camels, and followed the man: and the servant took Rebekah, and went his way.*

Rebekah said, "I will go." If she had not been willing to go back with Abraham's servant, would the will of God have been stopped? Would the promise of God not have been manifested? We know that God can't lie, because once He has spoken something, it must come to pass. But maybe it would not have come through Rebekah. Please don't let your destiny be given to another. Do not give it up. Know you are chosen, and be willing to go.

Sister, now that you know you are chosen by the Lord and are not second choice, or that it did not happen out of some coincidence, there is still one lie you need to deal with. Do not be fooled into thinking the enemy does not know you are chosen. He does know, and he will continue to try to unseat you and get you off focus. He knows that God chose you and that you are anointed to be a helpmeet. He even knows you were chosen for a purpose. So the only thing he can do is play with your mind. The enemy will use anything and anyone to discredit you. Even the chosen have adversaries. There is still opposition. Sometimes opposition comes from those closest to you, maybe even family members. But we are going to kill that spirit today! You are chosen, and you will not be unseated.

What about when family members try to plant a seed of doubt in you? Let's look at the book of Numbers, 12:1 says, *"And Miriam and Aaron spake against Moses because of the Ethiopian woman whom he had married: for he had married an Ethiopian woman."* The text is describing an account where Miriam and Aaron were speaking against their brother Moses concerning his choice of a wife. We know that Moses had married one of the daughters of Jethro. Exodus 2:16 says, *"Now the priest of Midian had seven daughters: and they came and drew [water], and filled the troughs to water their father's flock"*; and Exodus 2:21 says, *"And Moses was content to dwell with the man: and he gave Moses Zipporah his daughter."* Some believe that maybe Moses took another wife, but the Bible does not record this. We are not going to discuss which wife Miriam and Aaron spoke about. But the question is, were they correct in their rebuke of Moses? Were they correct in questioning Moses' choice for a wife? I believe this was merely a smokescreen to attack Moses in other areas. But let's deal with the attack of the wife first.

I believe this was an attempt to cripple Moses' wife by making her believe something was wrong with her, making her believe she was not good enough, making her believe her family was not good enough, and making her believe her background was not good enough. You see, the enemy uses words to plant seeds of doubt, seeds of low self-esteem, and seeds of self-hatred. To tell you the truth, sometimes things are said about us, and it is not that we agree with them but rather that we do not disagree with them. Instead, we let that small lie attach itself to our spirit instead of immediately rebuking the words and the spirit attached to the words.

These words then take root in our spirit and grow like a cancerous vine that spreads until it chokes out every good thought we have of ourselves. Then, when it is time for us to operate in our called purpose, we cannot operate fully because that cancerous vine has begun to bear the fruit of low self-esteem, no self-confidence, self-hatred, and self-loathing.

You see, with the seeds of doubt planted and growing, Moses' wife would never have been able to fully operate in the calling of wife. She would always have the thought planted by Miriam and Aaron. She would always wonder if she were chosen by God to be his wife, just as some have tried to do with us. But the devil is still a liar.

You see, in this scenario, the enemy uses us to stop us, or should I say uses you to stop you. But you can plead the blood of Jesus over this lying, accusatory demon, in the name of Jesus. And you can rebuke the spirit of self-hatred and low self-esteem now by the authority given by God through Christ Jesus. So rise up, for God has chosen you!

Now let's get into this brother-sister thing, the real reason for the attack. The plain truth is that there are going to be times when the enemy tries to use you to attack your husband. I can't say it any more clearly than that. You have to know who you are and who chose you so that when lies and accusations come, you will be able to stand. Aaron and Miriam were Moses' brother and sister. If anyone should have seen the hand of God on Moses' life, they should have. Right! Well, do not be surprised when those closest to you don't respect the call of God on your life.

Look at what God had already done in Moses' life. It was God who kept His hand on Moses. It was God who spared his life as a baby. It was God who watched over him while he grew in Pharaoh's house. It was God who kept him when he fled Egypt. It was God who brought him to Jethro's wells, and it was God who chose Moses to return and deliver the people of Israel from their bondage in Egypt. So the question is, why would his sister and brother question his choice of a wife now? Or were they really questioning God? Was the motive behind the question really jealousy?

The text brings us to the point where Miriam and Aaron were speaking against Moses because of the Ethiopian woman he had married. I don't think they wanted to talk about the wife at all. I believe she was just being used as a door to what they really wanted to confront Moses about. Check out the text: they went straight to Moses and his relationship with God.

You see, in this scenario, Moses' wife was just being used. But even when we as wives are being used, it still hurts. Any woman, but in this instance, Moses' wife, hearing those negative words would most likely feel hurt and maybe wonder if they could be right. The Bible does not record Moses' wife defending herself. But look at her rescuer: God came to her defense and quieted the adversary.

Numbers 12:1–12 says:

And Miriam and Aaron spake against Moses because of the Ethiopian woman whom he had married: for

*he had married an Ethiopian woman. And they said,
Hath the LORD indeed spoken only by Moses? hath he
not spoken also by us? And the LORD heard it. (Now
the man Moses was very meek, above all the men
which were upon the face of the earth.) And the LORD
spake suddenly unto Moses, and unto Aaron, and
unto Miriam, Come out ye three unto the tabernacle
of the congregation. And they three came out. And
the LORD came down in the pillar of the cloud, and
stood in the door of the tabernacle, and called Aaron
and Miriam: and they both came forth. And he said,
Hear now my words: If there be a prophet among
you, I the LORD will make myself known unto him in
a vision, and will speak unto him in a dream. My servant Moses is not so, who is faithful in all mine house.
With him will I speak mouth to mouth, even appar-
ently, and not in dark speeches; and the similitude of
the LORD shall he behold: wherefore then were ye not
afraid to speak against my servant Moses? And the
anger of the LORD was kindled against them; and he
departed. And the cloud departed from off the tabernacle; and, behold, Miriam became leprous, white as
snow: and Aaron looked upon Miriam, and, behold,
she was leprous.*

So stay encouraged as God chooses you. Don't worry;
stay in the will of God. He will be your defender and answer
every adversary for you. Note that the text does not record
Moses' wife ever answering Miriam or Aaron, but it does
show God's answer.

God always has a choice: His divine will for us. And
because of the nature of God, we know His choice is the best
choice. Stand strong in knowing you were chosen. But know
that you were chosen of God to walk through life with your
husband.

Chapter 4

Chosen for the Call

Chapter Prayer

Thank You, God, for choosing me.
Even before I knew You, You chose me!
God, thank You for the plans You have for me.
Thank You that I am favored among women,
because You loved me so much as to put purpose
in my life.
Help me to understand that You chose me,
and Your choice is right.
God, help me to listen only to Your voice,
and then silence every tongue that would rise
against me and my purpose,
in the name of Jesus.

Help me to be willing and to yield myself to what
You have chosen me to do.
Help me to rebuke every lying tongue and every
accusing spirit, in the name of Jesus.
Expose and destroy every lie, God.
I bind the spirit of low self-esteem, self-hatred, low
self-confidence, and depression,
in the name of Jesus.
And I pray for self-confidence.
God, give me boldness.
God, teach me when and how to defend myself.
God, I put all my trust in You as my ultimate defender.
It is You who will defend Your choices for my life.
In the name of Jesus,
Amen.

Chapter 5

Help Can't Cover
ᕼᐤᕾ

Husband: the "house-band," connecting and
keeping together the whole family. A man, when
betrothed, was esteemed a husband from that
time forward.

Ephesians 5:23: *"For the husband is the head of the
wife, even as Christ is the head of the church; and
he is the savior of the body."*

1 Corinthians 11:3: *"But I would have you
know, that the head of every man is Christ; and
the head of the woman is the man; and the head
of Christ is God."*

A s we encourage and talk about what we are chosen by
God to do as wives (as helpmeets, suitable), it is just
as important, if not more so, to talk about what God has not
called us to be. The husband has been called and placed by
God in the position of covering. Ephesians 5:23 says, *"For
the husband is the head of the wife, even as Christ is the
head of the church; and he is the savior of the body."*

58

We have all been told God is a God of order. In His order, there are positions; and in each position, there is responsibility; and for each responsibility, there is accountability. Each partner in a marriage has different roles, which varies for each marriage. I will not say that there is an itemized list somewhere that lists what he does and what she does, because in this day and time, husbands and wives juggle tasks to accomplish each family's specific needs. So some wives choose to stay home while their children are small, some stay home but have offices at home, and some have jobs outside the home. The husband's role may have just as much variety as the wife's. So we cannot say which way is right for everyone. But I do feel the order of God does not change. We as wives must be careful not to emasculate our husbands just because our roles might not be traditional.

In Ephesians, Christ's position as the head of the church and Savior of the body is clear in both role and responsibility. Within the same verse, God calls the husband to take on the same role and responsibility with his wife in marriage. Now before we get started, I know some of you are saying, "But he needs my help to be the head." I do agree with you, but only in part. Our husbands do need our help in some things, but our husbands are the head, not because we help them, but because that is what God called them to be. You must ask the question, wouldn't God equip him with all he needs to be the head, since He is the one who called him? Furthermore, once God says that something is, it is. God has already called him the head of the wife. So you don't need to help him be the head. God has already positioned your husband as head. What you do is help him operate, function as head. The question we must ask ourselves here is "Does the church help Christ be the head?".

An oversimplified example would be if your husband has been called to the office of pastor. You can't help him be the pastor, but you can help him pastor or operate as pastor. You see, there is a difference here between the noun and the verb. This could mean you take care of more tasks at home, which frees him to spend more time to seek God and feed God's sheep. Or you may co-labor with him on a daily basis in the ministry. Maybe you take care of daily church operations in order to give him more time to seek God for leadership. You must understand you can't make him be a pastor or call him to the office of pastor. You cannot cover him as pastor. But you can help him to pastor.

When speaking of covering, maybe I should explain what is meant by that term. The husband should be the barrier through which the attacks of the enemy have to cross. The husband should be in such an intimate vertical relationship with his heavenly Father that he is the one to whom God gives direction for his family. The husband as covering is anointed to be the guardian, protector, and high priest. He is the priest and the prophet of his home, and although God does honor our position as wives, there are just some things our husbands can do because of their position.

Sometimes as helpers, we want those we love to succeed in everything they do, and we begin to help in areas God has not directed us to. As a result, our help becomes leading or controlling. Don't get me wrong; we wives are called by God to be helpmeets. But in all the help we give, let us pray first that we are helping in a good way. The one thing we should not do is to take on responsibilities God has not given us. This applies to all our relationships. These added responsibilities become our choices and works of the flesh.

One thing you must remember is that you cannot answer a spiritual call with a fleshly work. Because flesh begets flesh, you will always have to carry the flesh answer. I want to warn you ladies that you can't carry your husband. You're not his savior, and you will never be! Jesus was the only Savior for the body, and He died doing it. Do not call yourself to be anyone's savior or covering, you will regret it.

Although as helpmeets we cannot cover our husbands, we should always be ready and willing to help them in whatever God has spoken for them to accomplish. The Bible records Zipporah, the wife of Moses, helping him. Exodus 4:24–26 says, *"And it came to pass by the way in the inn, that the* Lord *met him, and sought to kill him. Then Zipporah took a sharp stone, and cut off the foreskin of her son, and cast it at his feet, and said, Surely a bloody husband art thou to me. So he let him go: then she said, A bloody husband thou art, because of the circumcision."*

When first reading this text, it seems like Zipporah came to the aid of her husband. But was she helping him after she tried to control him? Let's examine a possible explanation. Zipporah circumcised her son, which was an act that the father was supposed to do eight days after the child's birth. It seems that Moses had committed a sin of omission. He had forgotten or decided not to perform the circumcision of his son. The act of circumcision was an act done in remembrance of God's covenant with Abraham. The important question is, why? We probably could discuss this all day, because the Bible does not specify, but I would like to present one possible reason.

Moses had married Zipporah, who was not of Israel, although her father was Jethro, the priest of Midian. Could it have been that his wife did not want her sons circumcised? Did Moses make his choice of omission to satisfy his wife's desire? She may have been a loving mother who did not want her child put through this pain. Had her cries brought her husband and family to this point? Is this why she had to perform the circumcision: because she was the one who had opposed it? The Bible does not say.

God had said to circumcise the child, but how did she know this would save her husband's life? Had God required this of Moses, but he had not hearkened to the Lord? How did Zipporah know this would be acceptable by God? This is only my opinion, but what if her cries, desires, fears, and or traditions had caused her husband to not hear God? How many of us are guilty of the exact same thing? We as women can petition our husbands over and over again until sometimes they give in. We must always give them encouraging words to go forward, but always in the will of God.

In order that I do not put my own slant on the Word of God, we must also explore the possibility that Zipporah was a faithful wife who came to her husband's aid. It could be that Zipporah, in the moment she saw her husband almost slain by God, remembered God's earlier commandment, and the circumcision was her attempt to please God. The Bible is not clear, but we must always be found helping rather than hindering our husbands.

Our next example of a woman helping her husband to the point of control is a biblical personality most of us have heard of: Jezebel. Jezebel, the wife of Ahab, has been characterized by many in churchdom as a harlot and a loose woman with provocative clothing and red-painted fingernails, but I want to encourage my sisters to read the Scriptures in 1 and 2 Kings. The Bible does not say these things. I would like to bring to light another point of view: maybe one of Jezebel's problems was that she helped to the point of taking control. You see, what we are talking about here is not visual appearance, but a spirit of taking over by means of manipulation, using deceit. So let's not talk about what she looked like or the clothing she wore.

Jezebel was a queen; she had been raised as the daughter of a king, Ethbaal, king of the Zidonians. Jezebel probably lived her entire life with the finest of things and was probably trained to carry herself as a queen. So this misconception of her being trash, a cheap woman with painted fingernails and short dresses, may not be exactly correct or the entire truth. One of Jezebel's main problems was that in attempting to help her husband, she began to control and then lead him.

Jezebel's actions were led by a spirit of control and manipulation. This Jezebel spirit seeks to come in under the guise of helping but begins leading and controlling.

An important side comment for all of us to remember is that the spirit of Jezebel hates the true prophets of God. The Jezebel spirit seeks to kill the prophet. You see, a true prophet brings the people direction and guidance from God. God would then be in control, and the spirit of Jezebel could no longer control the situation with deception and manipulation. So it would rather kill the truth than to relinquish control.

Be mindful, ladies, that this spirit does not rise up in you. The last thing you want to do is "kill" the priest of your home, the man God has sent as your husband, the band around your home, the prophet of your home. As we begin reading about Jezebel, I want you to ask yourself the question, "Is a little bit of this Jezebel spirit, that spirit of control, in me?"

As we begin reading our text, we see that Ahab began to reign as king and had already begun doing evil in the sight of the Lord, before he married Jezebel. First Kings 16:28–33 says:

So Omri slept with his fathers, and was buried in Samaria: and Ahab his son reigned in his stead. And in the thirty and eighth year of Asa king of Judah began Ahab the son of Omri to reign over Israel: and Ahab the son of Omri reigned over Israel in Samaria twenty and two years. And Ahab the son of Omri did evil in the sight of the LORD above all that were before him. And it came to pass, as if it had been a light thing for him to walk in the sins of Jeroboam the son of Nebat, that he took to wife Jezebel the daughter of Ethbaal king of the Zidonians, and went and served Baal, and worshipped him. And he reared up an altar for Baal in the house of Baal, which he had built in Samaria. And Ahab made a grove; and Ahab did

*more to provoke the LORD God of Israel to anger than
all the kings of Israel that were before him.*

Another of the charges against Jezebel is that she stirred
up her husband's evildoing. She helped him to do what was
wrong in the sight of God. In 1 Kings 19:1–3, when Ahab
complained to Jezebel concerning the prophets, not only
did Jezebel help, but she also took over and led the persecu-
tion of the prophet of the Lord. But Ahab was already per-
secuting the prophets. As 1 Kings 19:1–3 says, "*And Ahab
told Jezebel all that Elijah had done, and withal how he had
slain all the prophets with the sword. Then Jezebel sent a
messenger unto Elijah, saying, So let the gods do to me, and
more also, if I make not thy life as the life of one of them by to
morrow about this time. And when he saw that, he arose, and
went for his life, and came to Beersheba, which belongeth to
Judah, and left his servant there.*"

You see, it was not that Ahab was turned from God; he
had already done evil in the sight of God before he married
Jezebel. My question here is, what if she could have influenced Ahab to turn back to God? What if Jezebel had tried
to turn her husband back to God? What if she had tried to
encourage him to obey God's commandments? This question, of course, cannot be answered in Ahab's case. But what
about yours? Are you encouraging your husband to draw
closer to God, or are you leading him away from Him?

Another example of Jezebel's control is found in the story
about a vineyard Ahab wanted. First Kings 21:1–16 says:

*And it came to pass after these things, that
Naboth the Jezreelite had a vineyard, which was in
Jezreel, hard by the palace of Ahab king of Samaria.
And Ahab spake unto Naboth, saying, Give me thy
vineyard, that I may have it for a garden of herbs,
because it is near unto my house: and I will give thee*

for it a better vineyard than it; or, if it seem good to thee, I will give thee the worth of it in money. And Naboth said to Ahab, The LORD forbid it me, that I should give the inheritance of my fathers unto thee.

And Ahab came into his house heavy and displeased because of the word which Naboth the Jezreelite had spoken to him: for he had said, I will not give thee the inheritance of my fathers. And he laid him down upon his bed, and turned away his face, and would eat no bread. But Jezebel his wife came to him, and said unto him, Why is thy spirit so sad, that thou eatest no bread? And he said unto her, Because I spake unto Naboth the Jezreelite, and said unto him, Give me thy vineyard for money; or else, if it please thee, I will give thee another vineyard for it: and he answered, I will not give thee my vineyard. And Jezebel his wife said unto him, Dost thou now govern the kingdom of Israel? arise, and eat bread, and let thine heart be merry: I will give thee the vineyard of Naboth the Jezreelite. So she wrote letters in Ahab's name, and sealed them with his seal, and sent the letters unto the elders and to the nobles that were in his city, dwelling with Naboth. And she wrote in the letters, saying, Proclaim a fast, and set Naboth on high among the people: And set two men, sons of Belial, before him, to bear witness against him, saying, Thou didst blaspheme God and the king. And then carry him out, and stone him, that he may die. And the men of his city, even the elders and the nobles who were the inhabitants in his city, did as Jezebel had sent unto them, and as it was written in the letters which she had sent unto them. They proclaimed a fast, and set Naboth on high among the people. And there came in two men, children of Belial, and sat before him: and the men of Belial witnessed against him, even against Naboth, in the presence of the people, saying, Naboth did blaspheme God and the king. Then they carried him forth out of the city, and stoned him with stones, that he died. Then they sent to Jezebel, saying, Naboth is stoned, and is dead. And it came to pass, when Jezebel heard that Naboth was stoned, and was dead, that Jezebel said to Ahab, Arise, take possession of the vineyard of Naboth the Jezreelite, which he refused to give thee for money: for Naboth is not alive, but dead. And it came to pass, when Ahab heard that Naboth was dead, that Ahab rose up to go down to the vineyard of Naboth the Jezreelite, to take possession of it.

Jezebel not only took control from Ahab, but she also forged a letter, devised lies, manipulated men, and authored a murder plot. All this was done to circumvent the will of God. The end result was her husband was given what he wanted, and she was in the driver's seat as she wanted.

This is an extreme example for many of us. I am sure we do not want to compare ourselves to the horrible Jezebel! But my question to all of us is, is there anything in the illustration that we mimic in our own lives? Have we taken control of any situation through manipulation, and are we operating in the flesh to accomplish our will? The dangerous thing about taking control is that God will call all of us to give an account for our actions. And ladies, even though we may think we are helping our husbands, God will hold us in account for all we do in His sight. So be careful of what you take on and what you do.

As a result of all Jezebel's manipulation, her fate was sealed by God. Look at how God judged Jezebel and Ahab. First Kings 21:21–25 says:

Behold, I will bring evil upon thee, and will take away thy posterity, and will cut off from Ahab him that pisseth against the wall, and him that is shut up and left in Israel, And will make thine house like the house of Jeroboam the son of Nebat, and like the house of Baasha the son of Ahijah, for the provocation where-with thou hast provoked me to anger, and made Israel to sin. And of Jezebel also spake the LORD, saying, The dogs shall eat Jezebel by the wall of Jezreel. Him that dieth of Ahab in the city the dogs shall eat; and him that dieth in the field shall the fowls of the air eat. But there was none like unto Ahab, which did sell himself to work wickedness in the sight of the LORD, whom Jezebel his wife stirred up.

The text talks about Jezebel's fate and the reason for her sentence: she had stirred up Ahab's wickedness. Sometimes we read this text and become self-righteous to the point that we do not believe we are as bad as the wicked Jezebel. But my question here is, have you stirred up anything in your husband?

Do you need some examples? Well, I am glad you asked! What about when your husband is frustrated at work? Do you encourage him to remain peaceful, keep his witness, and seek God for the next step? Or do you get as frustrated as he is and tell him he should go and tell them all off? Okay, what if your husband feels God has called him to preach, but because of where God has planted your family, it appears that the opportunity to preach is rare? Do you tell him to leave where you are and start his own church without con-sulting God or his spiritual covering? These are my exam-ples. What are yours? These questions deserve an answer. Take a moment and answer, what are you stirring up in your husband?

The consequences of Ahab and Jezebel's actions are recorded in 2 Kings 9:1–37. I encourage you to read it. We are going to pick up the text at 2 Kings 9:30:

And when Jehu was come to Jezreel, Jezebel heard of it; and she painted her face, and tired her head, and looked out at a window. And as Jehu entered in at the gate, she said, Had Zimri peace, who slew his master? And he lifted up his face to the window, and said, Who is on my side? who? And there looked out to him two or three eunuchs. And he said, Throw her down. So they threw her down: and some of her blood was sprinkled on the wall, and on the horses: and he trode her under foot. And when he was come in, he did eat and drink, and said, Go, see now this cursed woman, and bury her: for she is a king's daughter. And they went to bury her: but they found no more of her than the skull, and the feet, and the palms of her hands. Wherefore they came again, and told him. And he said, This is the word of the LORD, which he spake by his servant Elijah the Tishbite, saying, In the portion of Jezreel shall dogs eat the flesh of Jezebel: And the carcase of Jezebel shall be as dung upon the face of the field in the portion of Jezreel; so that they shall not say, This is Jezebel.

Jezebel's fate is also recorded in Revelation 2:20–21: *"Notwithstanding I have a few things against thee, because thou sufferest that woman Jezebel, which calleth herself a prophetess, to teach and to seduce my servants to commit fornication, and to eat things sacrificed unto idols. And I gave her space to repent of her fornication; and she repented not."*

So sister, even if you started out with good intentions but have become controlling, I urge you to repent. Ask God and your husband for forgiveness. And remember, help can't cover.

Chapter 5

Help Can't Cover

Chapter Prayer

God, I thank You for my husband!
God, I thank You because he is my covering.
God, I thank You because he is the priest of my home.
God, I thank You because You placed him in the
office of husband.
God, I thank You that my husband
is the smartest and most anointed man to make the
decisions for my household.
God, I thank You for giving my husband wisdom to
lead our household.
God, help me now to be the wife You ordained for
me to be.
God, help me to help my husband according to Your will.
God, I don't want to control my husband.
God, I don't want to manipulate my husband.
God, if there is anything in me that seeks to control,
if there is anything in me that seeks to lead or cover,
remove it from me.
God, if there is anything in me that would
manipulate circumstances
and people to get my desired outcome,
I pray You remove it from me now,
in the name of Jesus.
Help me, God, to submit to Your order,
submit to your plan,
and submit to Your will,
in the name of Jesus.
Amen.

Chapter 6

Careful What You Give Him
᎙ᏺ

Genesis 3:17–19: *"And unto Adam he said, Because thou hast hearkened unto the voice of thy wife, ... cursed is the ground for thy sake; in sorrow shalt thou eat of it all the days of thy life; Thorns also and thistles shall it bring forth to thee; and thou shalt eat the herb of the field; In the sweat of thy face shalt thou eat bread, till thou return unto the ground; for out of it wast thou taken: for dust thou art, and unto dust shalt thou return."*

Genesis 16:2–3: *"And Sarai said unto Abram, ….. I pray thee, go in unto my maid; …... And Abram hearkened to the voice of Sarai. ..., and gave her to her husband Abram to be his wife.*

Now we are going to really get into your business! What have you been giving your husband? What have you been giving him in the area of counsel on spiritual matters? I am not talking about when everything is fine and all the bills are paid, or when the children are being obedient and making straight As in school. I am not talking about when you or he has just received a promotion and a large salary increase. I am not talking about when you have just lost five inches and went down two dress sizes. No, that is definitely not what I am talking about.

I am talking about when he is tired, you are tired, and God's Word is seeming to tarry a little too long. I am talking about when God has said He will bring you out, but there is no sign of God working anywhere. I am talking about when no bills are paid, your husband is out of work, or maybe both of you are out of work. I am talking about when you are facing foreclosure or contemplating filing bankruptcy, or maybe your car was just repossessed. I am talking about when it seems as though God is not coming through but the contrary is happening, when everything you thought you had is either leaving or being taken away. I am talking about when friends and family are becoming more distant, and there is no one to talk to. What are you saying? What are the comments made under your breath? What is your body language saying? What are you calling your husband? What are you saying to him about God? What are you saying to him about his ministry now? Come on, let's all come clean. What are you giving your husband?

Well, in this chapter, we are going to hit it all. And this is a chapter you are really going to have to use to examine yourself by the Word of God and change! God's Word says in Proverbs 18:21, *"Death and life are in the power of the tongue: and they that love it shall eat the fruit thereof."* So let's see how we have been using the power of the tongue.

In Genesis 3:17, God said, *"And unto Adam he said, Because thou hast hearkened unto the voice of thy wife . . ."* This Scripture comes immediately after the fall of man, and God is telling Adam and Eve the consequences of their disobedience. The words "Because thou hast hearkened to the voice of thy wife" could be one of the best statements God could say concerning us as wives, or it could be the worst. It could bring honor or shame. Can you imagine your husband making a wrong choice, and when God comes to judge him, God uses these words concerning you—not that your husband just made a wrong choice, but that your voice was instrumental in his wrong choice? You used your voice to convince him to make this choice. You influenced him. You "helped" him make the wrong choice.

The question I want you to ask yourself as you read is, can God trust you to talk to your husband? Can He trust you to give to your husband? Will you give him godly counsel, support, and encouragement? Will you help him and yourself as God molds and shapes your lives for His glory? Can God trust your voice, your tongue?

I am not trying to say that we won't make mistakes. We do make wrong choices sometimes. But there are times we allow emotions to cloud our judgment. We tend to lean more to what we feel and forget what we know God has said. Sometimes we pay more attention to what things appear to be while forsaking what God is doing in the unseen, in the spirit. And because of our feelings and what we do see in the natural, sometimes we give to our husbands what seems to be a good idea (or good in our sight), but it may not be the God idea for us. The result of this good idea may oftentimes be a product of the flesh. And because we authored it, we must carry it. The good idea soon becomes a burden instead of a blessing. The result of a good idea may also be outside the will of God, and although we believe we are helping, in reality we are hurting ourselves and others.

Let's look at some examples of women who gave to their husbands and then bring it to our day. Of course, we are going to start with the beginning, Eve and her infamous giving to her husband, Adam. The Bible records in Genesis 3:6, *"And when the woman saw that the tree was good for food, and that it was pleasant to the eyes, and a tree to be desired to make one wise, she took of the fruit thereof, and did eat, and gave also unto her husband with her; and he did eat."*

Of course, every woman says if she had been Eve, she would have obeyed God without question. She would have known better and on and on, and she would not have given Adam anything from the tree. But the truth is, if we are honest, we really don't know what we would have done. I do not want it to appear that Eve was correct in giving Adam of the tree, but in her defense, let's look at exactly what the Bible records and maybe get more understanding of why Eve did what she did, even why we give our husbands ideas that seem good.

The Bible says Eve looked at the fruit as something good. She looked and found it pleasant to the eyes. Eve saw the fruit as desirable to make one wise. It appears from the text that Eve thought the fruit was good to give to her husband. Now let's think about Eve's position. She had just had a conversation with the serpent, and because of his subtle lies, she saw the fruit differently. The serpent had subtly changed Eve's view of the fruit. He deceived her to the point where it seemed to be a good thing, that it could not possibly be wrong to eat of it.

I imagine Eve began to reason within herself: Okay, this tree looks good, its fruit looks good for food, and on top of all this, it will increase our wisdom. How could God not want my husband and me to have this good thing? In her mind, Eve convinced herself that a seemingly good thing was a God thing. As a result, she ate and gave it to her husband also. My question to you is, what have you been looking at a little differently, convincing yourself that it is okay to do, convincing yourself that it is okay to say? Forget Eve, just look inside yourself. What are you choosing today? What are you using the power of your tongue to promote? See, it's easy to examine Eve, but let's examine ourselves.

I am not saying that either Adam or Eve was totally responsible for the other's actions, but sometimes we can cause our husbands to believe in a lie. As a result, it will cause a fall, and we must take responsibility for that. We are not going to argue in this book about whose fault it was or who was to blame, but we are going to concentrate only on Eve's role. The one thing I want us to see is that God did not just say, "Because thou hast eaten of the tree"; but God also said, "Because thou hast hearkened to the voice of thy wife."

See, God judged Adam because he listened to Eve. God could have judged only Adam's action of eating from the tree, but why did He also include *"Because thou hast hearkened unto the voice of thy wife"* (Gen. 3:17)? I would like to suggest that was added for us as wives. Imagine standing with your husband before God, with your husband, the man you love, the man you want to see blessed, the man whom you want to realize his purpose in God, and now God has to deal with him because of something you suggested, pushed, promoted, maybe even cried about over and over and over again. I know; he did not have to listen to you, but he did!

We know what happened next, but you can read it for yourself in Genesis 3:7–16. Let's skip to the seventeenth verse. The Scripture records in Genesis 3:17–19: *"And unto Adam he said, Because thou hast hearkened unto the voice of thy wife, and hast eaten of the tree, of which I commanded thee, saying, Thou shalt not eat of it: cursed is the ground for thy sake; in sorrow shalt thou eat of it all the days of thy life; Thorns also and thistles shall it bring forth to thee; and thou shalt eat the herb of the field; In the sweat of thy face shalt thou eat bread, till thou return unto the ground; for out of it wast thou taken: for dust thou art, and unto dust shalt thou return."* We need to realize all of mankind was affected because Adam hearkened to the voice of his wife.

You see, we women do have our ways when we want something, and they are not all to our credit. We sow seeds of manipulation so our husbands can see our points of view and receive our "good" ideas. Okay, you don't have to agree.

What about those small, subtle gifts of attitude, sucking teeth, rolling eyes, silent treatments, oh, and let's not forget the tears or "closing up shop." The truth is, there is no room for manipulation in a marriage. No one can live with constant badgering.

On the note of badgering, I want to explore Proverbs 21:9. It says, *"It is better to dwell in a corner of the housetop, than with a brawling woman in a wide house."* Imagine living in a home spacious and filled with every luxury imaginable. Every room has been decorated to your specific taste; you choose the furniture, carpet, window treatments, everything down to just the right pictures and framing. Now imagine that this house impeccably decorated is ready for guests. The floor plan is open and designed specifically for entertaining family and friends. But to add the icing to the cake, you have a raving woman running through the house screaming at everyone. She is unhappy and expressing it often. She expresses it to you, the children, the guests, and anyone walking by. Now you realize that nothing can really be said to pacify her. You decide not to argue back, but because of her actions, your children are scared, and your family and friends would not come over even if you begged. Instead of arguing or leaving the house, maybe to some more inviting company, you find a quiet space and hold on to whatever peace you still can find.

How would this make you feel? You wouldn't be able to enjoy the blessing of your house. You wouldn't have the comfort of your home. The security and stability of your children would be in jeopardy, and no one who knows the woman would dare come over. How do you feel? What do you want to happen? What do you want God to do? Now imagine you are the ranting woman, and your husband is caught in the house. Hm-m-m . . .

Since we are out here, I want to hit another one. Proverbs 21:19 says, *"It is better to dwell in the wilderness, than with a contentious and an angry woman."* Should we go any further? I am not sure. I can't take this myself! Imagine your husband would rather leave the comforts of your home and go out into the wilderness, a dry unfruitful place with no comfort of home! He would rather live in these conditions than to live in the same house with you. So the question you must ask yourself is whether you are becoming bitter and angry. Are you a contentious woman? Are you tearing down your home? Are you damaging your children? Think about it, because you need to give an honest answer.

We want to always build our homes, not run our husbands away. Please do not misunderstand me; I believe that our opinions do matter, and we do have a right to voice our needs, hurts, and desires. But how are we voicing these opinions? Even the strongest of men can be brought to change because of the petitioning of a woman.

Okay, I can tell you need some more convincing, so let's look at Samson. Often we talk about Delilah and Samson and skip Samson's wife. Samson had problems with a couple of women in his life. Let's read Judges 14:17–19:

> *And she wept before him the seven days, while their feast lasted: and it came to pass on the seventh day, that he told her, because she lay sore upon him: and she told the riddle to the children of her people. And the men of the city said unto him on the seventh day before the sun went down, What is sweeter than honey? and what is stronger than a lion? And he said unto them, If ye had not plowed with my heifer, ye had not found out my riddle. And the Spirit of the LORD came upon him, and he went down to Ashkelon, and slew thirty men of them, and took their spoil, and gave change of garments unto them which expounded the riddle. And his anger was kindled, and he went up to his father's house.*

Here Samson was at his wedding feast with his new bride, and she began to question him for an answer to a riddle. She had been coerced by her people into finding out the answer from her new husband. She had no loyalty to her new husband and used whatever resources to get what she wanted. She did not even seem to care about the cost to her husband. She began to cry. As a matter of a fact, she cried for seven days. Can you imagine crying, pouting, and having an attitude for seven days? No, of course not you, her!

After this incident, you would think Samson would have reconsidered telling a woman his secrets. At least, not the mysteries given to him by God. But we know the account of Samson and Delilah (Judges 16:1–31). Sometimes we women use even our families to get what we want by whatever manipulative means possible.

How about one more example? Can we stand it? King Herod's account is listed in Mark 6:17–28:

For Herod himself had sent forth and laid hold upon John, and bound him in prison for Herodias' sake, his brother Philip's wife: for he had married her. For John had said unto Herod, It is not lawful for thee to have thy brother's wife. Therefore Herodias had a quarrel against him, and would have killed him; but she could not: For Herod feared John, knowing that he was a just man and an holy, and observed him; and when he heard him, he did many things, and heard him gladly.

And when a convenient day was come, that Herod on his birthday made a supper to his lords, high captains, and chief estates of Galilee; And when the daughter of the said Herodias came in, and danced, and pleased Herod and them that sat with him, the king said unto the damsel, Ask of me whatsoever thou wilt, and I will give it thee. And he sware unto her, Whatsoever thou shalt ask of me, I will give it thee, unto the half of my kingdom. And she went forth, and said unto her mother, What shall I ask? And she said, The head of John the Baptist. And she came in straightway with haste unto the king, and asked, saying, I will that thou give me by and by in a charger the head of John the Baptist. And the king was exceeding sorry; yet for his oath's sake, and for their sakes which sat with him, he would not reject her. And immediately the king sent an executioner, and commanded his head to be brought: and he went and beheaded him in the prison, And brought his head in a charger, and gave it to the damsel: and the damsel gave it to her mother.

As also recorded in Matthew 14:3–11:

For Herod had laid hold on John, and bound him, and put him in prison for Herodias' sake, his brother Philip's wife. For John said unto him, It is not lawful for thee to have her. And when he would have put him to death, he feared the multitude, because they counted him as a prophet. But when Herod's birthday was kept, the daughter of Herodias danced before them, and pleased Herod. Whereupon he promised with an oath to give her whatsoever she would ask. And she, being before instructed of her mother, said, Give me here John Baptist's head in a charger. And the king was sorry: nevertheless for the oath's sake, and them which sat with him at meat, he commanded it to be given her. And he sent, and beheaded John in the prison. And his head was brought in a charger, and given to the damsel: and she brought it to her mother.

Herod was king, yet his wife used a damsel, a young girl who danced for him, to get what she wanted. Think about it, ladies. She only danced! Herodias gave her daughter to get what she wanted. Hence, we want to make sure we are not using our children and family members to manipulate our husbands. Remember, the devil will use whomever he can.

You see, a wife's voice was meant to help and encourage her Adam. But that same voice can be used to make suggestions or encouragements that are not the will of God. Do you realize that the first act recorded about Eve was of her trying to please her husband while displeasing God? Ladies, we must always please God first in everything we do, and as a result, our husbands will be blessed. I must admit, the last thing I want God to say to my husband is that He is judging him because of something I suggested he do.

Let's go further with another example of a wife giving to her husband. I like this one, because we often judge the wife, Sarai, so harshly. Sarai, whose husband was Abram, also had a "good" idea to help her husband reach his purpose in God. Let's read the text.

Genesis 16:1–3 says, *"Now Sarai Abram's wife bare him no children: and she had a handmaid, an Egyptian, whose name was Hagar. And Sarai said unto Abram, Behold now, the LORD hath restrained me from bearing: I pray thee, go in unto my maid; it may be that I may obtain children by her. And Abram hearkened to the voice of Sarai. And Sarai Abram's wife took Hagar her maid the Egyptian, after Abram had dwelt ten years in the land of Canaan, and gave her to her husband Abram to be his wife."*

Now before we get started, let's look at the time and the culture. Sarai was a woman who had not yet borne any children. During this time, for a woman not to have a child was likened to a curse; also, during this time, polygamy was lawful. Oftentimes a woman who could not have children would allow her maidservant to marry her husband in an attempt to have a child.

This was also recorded of Rachel in Genesis 30:1–5: *"And when Rachel saw that she bare Jacob no children, Rachel envied her sister; and said unto Jacob, Give me children, or else I die. And Jacob's anger was kindled against Rachel: and he said, Am I in God's stead, who hath withheld from thee the fruit of the womb? And she said, Behold my maid Bilhah, go in unto her; and she shall bear upon my knees, that I may also have children by her. And she gave him Bilhah her handmaid to wife: and Jacob went in unto her. And Bilhah conceived, and bare Jacob a son."*

We see that in the culture of the time, Sarai's actions were normal practice or, should I say, what was considered lawful. What we have to be cautious of as wives is doing something that is accepted by society, but out of the will of God. One example would be to get a second job to have more money instead of paying our tithes and offerings from our first job and trusting God. Or we might marry someone because he appears to be the best we can get, or we buy the first house available in our budget because we do not trust God for anything better. Or maybe God promised us a house, so we go and borrow money from family members who will later talk about us, instead of trusting Him for the down payment or even to give us a house without the need for a down payment. So let's not judge Sarai too harshly for doing then what we are guilty of doing now.

See, the truth is, Sarai's problem then and our problem now are probably more similar than what we would like to admit. The bottom line is, when God says something but it seems impossible or as if He has forgotten, we often decide to help God, as though He needs our help. And as a result, we mess up and suffer the consequences. Then we must repent before God and wait on Him to fix our mess. Maybe you don't want to admit it, but as you read the passage, ask God to show you yourself. Ask yourself whether God has ever promised you and your husband something and you gave your voice to influence the outcome.

The account of Abram and Sarai begins in Genesis 12 and goes through Genesis 18; I encourage you to read the entire account. God gave Abram a promise at age seventy-five. Genesis 12:3–4 says, *"And I will bless them that bless thee, and curse him that curseth thee: and in thee shall all families of the earth be blessed. So Abram departed, as the LORD had spoken unto him; and Lot went with him: and Abram was seventy and five years old when he departed out of Haran."*

God spoke the promise to Abram again with detail. Genesis 15:1–6 continues:

After these things the word of the LORD came unto Abram in a vision, saying, Fear not, Abram: I am thy shield, and thy exceeding great reward. And Abram said, Lord GOD, what wilt thou give me, seeing I go childless, and the steward of my house is this Eliezer of Damascus? And Abram said, Behold, to me thou hast given no seed: and, lo, one born in my house is mine heir. And, behold, the word of the LORD came unto him, saying, This shall not be thine heir; but he that shall come forth out of thine own bowels shall be thine heir. And he brought him forth abroad, and said, Look now toward heaven, and tell the stars, if thou be able to number them: and he said unto him, So shall thy seed be. And he believed in the LORD; and he counted it to him for righteousness.

One chapter later, we read that Abram had a child with the handmaid given to him by Sarai. Genesis 16:15–16 says, *"And Hagar bare Abram a son: and Abram called his son's name, which Hagar bare, Ishmael. And Abram was fourscore* and six years old, when Hagar bare Ishmael to Abram." Then, Genesis 17:1–2 says, *"And when Abram was ninety years old and nine, the LORD appeared to Abram, and said unto him, I am the Almighty God; walk before me, and be thou perfect. And I will make my covenant between me and thee, and will multiply thee exceedingly."*

God spoke the promise yet once more; now He called out Sarah. God explained the child would come through Sarah. Genesis 17:16–19 says:

> *And I will bless her, and give thee a son also of her: yea, I will bless her, and she shall be a mother of nations; kings of people shall be of her. Then Abraham fell upon his face, and laughed, and said in his heart, Shall a child be born unto him that is an hundred years old? and shall Sarah, that is ninety years old, bear? And Abraham said unto God, O that Ishmael might live before thee! And God said, Sarah thy wife shall bear thee a son indeed; and thou shalt call his name Isaac: and I will establish my covenant with him for an everlasting covenant, and with his seed after him. But my covenant will I establish with Isaac, which Sarah shall bear unto thee at this set time in the next year.*

Sarah was visited by angels. Genesis 18:9–14 records the event:

> *And they said unto him, Where is Sarah thy wife? And he said, Behold, in the tent. And he said, I will certainly return unto thee according to the time of life; and, lo, Sarah thy wife shall have a son. And Sarah heard it in the tent door, which was behind him. Now Abraham and Sarah were old and well stricken in age; and it ceased to be with Sarah after the manner*

of women. Therefore Sarah laughed within herself, saying, After I am waxed old shall I have pleasure, my lord being old also? And the LORD said unto Abraham, Wherefore did Sarah laugh, saying, Shall I of a surety bear a child, which am old? Is any thing too hard for the LORD? At the time appointed I will return unto thee, according to the time of life, and Sarah shall have a son.

Genesis 21:1–5 states: *"And the LORD visited Sarah as he had said, and the LORD did unto Sarah as he had spoken. For Sarah conceived, and bare Abraham a son in his old age, at the set time of which God had spoken to him. And Abraham called the name of his son that was born unto him, whom Sarah bare to him, Isaac. And Abraham circumcised his son Isaac being eight days old, as God had commanded him. And Abraham was an hundred years old, when his son Isaac was born unto him."*

This illustration should encourage us all to wait on God to bring His promises to pass. But think about this: the consequences of Sarai's "good" idea, the child Ishmael, stayed with her the remainder of her life—in fact, even until this day. Talk about a choice impacting the world!

By Sarai's choice, Hagar was brought into the promise. Hagar makes me think about family members; although she was not a blood relative, she had been with Sarai for ten years. So Sarai had to think highly of her to suggest her as Abram's wife and to bear him a child. But take note of the consequences: a child of the promise versus a child of the flesh. So keep girlfriends, coworkers, family, and friends out of the promise God has spoken, and give your husband only godly counsel.

The warning is that if we choose "good" ideas instead of God ideas and give them to our husbands, it may not stop the perfect will of God, but we may have to live with the consequences, and not only us, but our children and even their children. Think about it: if Sarai had just encouraged Abram to wait on God, would the blessing have come sooner? There would have never been an Ishmael! What would our world be like today?

Women of God, remember that the words you give your husband are powerful. With your words, you can build your husband, shape your children, and encourage them to fight and love. So I encourage you not to sit silently by, but always be in prayer for your family, and let God anoint your words to bring life, not death, to your home.

Chapter 6

Careful What You Give Him

Chapter Prayer

Thank You, God, for Your Word.
And thank You, God, for showing me myself in Your Word.

God, please forgive me for using my words to tear
down my husband and my home.
God, forgive me for trying to give my husband
good ideas
that are contrary to Your will for our lives.
God, forgive me for trying to take control of our
situation without waiting on Your leading.
God, forgive me for trying to help You.

God, I ask You to show me how to help my husband
with my words.
Show me how to build my family, build my faith,
and give encouragement in the name of Jesus.
God, when my husband speaks vision,
help me to speak encouragement and agreement.
God, if he speaks doubt, help me to speak faith.

And with my words, teach me how to pray even
when I don't understand.
God, use me to be a suitable helpmeet in everything
I give my husband.
God, even our words shall be used to give You glory.

In the name of Jesus,
Amen.

Chapter 7

Presentation Is Everything
๑|๏

Esther 5:2–3: *"And it was so, when the king saw Esther the queen standing in the court, that she obtained favour in his sight: and the king held out to Esther the golden sceptre that was in his hand. So Esther drew near, and touched the top of the sceptre. Then said the king unto her, What wilt thou, queen Esther? and what is thy request? it shall be even given thee to the half of the kingdom."*

Now that we know what to give, Lord, help us give it right! Let's begin with how we have been giving in the past, because it will bring us to the concept of presentation.

Imagine that your husband brings you a gift. He walks over to you and throws a dirty, crumpled brown grocery bag. After he throws the bag towards you, he tells you, "Look what I had to bring you because you did not have sense enough to figure out that you needed a coat." You open the bag and find a beautiful mink coat. The coat is just your size and fits like a glove. It is warm, and you are positive it will keep you warm all winter. You love the gift, but what do you think about the presentation?

Now let's turn the table and ask ourselves how we are presenting our concerns, thoughts, and ideas to our husbands; especially when we may be correct and we know it. The way we question our husbands, confront them, and give them answers can make all the difference in the world, especially when we don't understand what God is doing with them. I am sure we ourselves want to be respected for what we believe God has said to us, even if no one else believes the promise God has made concerning us. We must also consider if we do the same thing for our spouses.

How do we communicate? Even when we are wrong, don't we want to be told we are wrong the right way? Sometimes as women, we want to be heard immediately, and sometimes we think we have the right to say whatever we want. But we need to be careful how we present our concerns, thoughts, and ideas.

I think that I can easily make the statement that there are going to be times in our lives when we are right and our husbands are wrong. But if we believe the husband is the head of the wife as Christ is the head of the church, then we must still respect God's order. And we must realize God will chastise His man! God cares so much about the wife. He wants us to be considered and cared for by our husbands.

To clarify my point, let's look at an illustration. Let's say we have a couple taking a leisurely drive. The husband is driving, and the wife is sitting in the passenger seat next to him. Imagine it is a spring day, and let's say they are driving in a little sports-car convertible. Let's make it a cute two seater . . . um-m-m . . . red. As they drive, they are talking about God and what He is doing in their lives. They are talking about purpose, destiny, and vision for their house. They are so relaxed. The husband is talking to his wife and occasionally glances in her direction. The wife suddenly notices a large truck approaching them, swerving, but just a little. The remainder of this story will follow one of three scenarios.

In the first scenario, the wife who sits next to her husband looks at the truck and does not say anything. She continues to talk to her husband as if nothing is wrong. She has her eyes on the approaching danger but never says a word. She does not know if her husband sees the truck wavering. She knows that this could be tragic, but she says nothing. She is thinking, What if I say something and I scare him? What if I say something and he already knows? What if he gets mad at me for saying something? Or she tells herself, He is driving; he does not need my help. So she just sits.

In the second scenario, the wife screams directly into her husband's ear and grabs the steering wheel with both hands. Her husband is startled by her actions. He takes one hand off the wheel to hold his now ringing ear. But when he takes one hand off the wheel, the car begins to spin because his wife is pulling the wheel with both her hands. The husband, who is now definitely not looking at the oncoming danger of the truck, still has no idea what his wife is screaming about. So now not only does he have the truck to worry about, but he also has to stop his car that is spinning because his wife pulled the steering wheel, all this and a panicking woman screaming in his ear!

In the third scenario, the wife sees the truck and looks at her husband to see if he sees it. She says one of her famous short prayers: "Help, Jesus!" Unsure of her husband's ability to see the truck, she slightly elevates her voice, keeps her composure, and alerts him about the oncoming swerving truck. She says, "Babe, do you see the swerving." Her husband answers her and adjusts his driving until the truck passes. The couple continues their drive.

Which wife are you? The fact here is that the couple could end this day that started out so peacefully in great tragedy or just as peacefully as it began. If the husband does not see the truck and does not turn the car in time, there will definitely be an accident. So what should we learn from each wife?

The first wife sees trouble, but says and does nothing. From her, we must learn to break the silence and talk to our husbands, especially if it seems danger may be approaching. We need to find time to speak with our husbands, if for nothing else than to ask, "How are you doing?" or "How do you feel?" We should not talk to them only in times of trouble, but always just to let them now we care about them. If the woman in the first scenario had just said something, the husband could have responded, "Yes, I am fine, but that truck is swerving."

The second wife is my favorite, probably because I am sometimes like her. She panics, and in her panic she causes more confusion. If you notice, she never actually warns her husband. She never helps him. Instead, she causes more confusion and panic.

The third wife is my role model. I want to be just like her when I grow up! She does not immediately panic, nor does she immediately try to tell her husband what to do. She just talks to God and then talks to her man. She does not cause more problems or more damage by panic and unnecessary anxiety, but she communicates in a manner where she can be understood and received. By no means does she, the anointed help, made-suitable help, brought-by-God help, sit there and do nothing. But the anointed helpmeet helps her husband in the right way. The presentation is everything!

Let's explore another illustration to extract keys on how we should communicate. Remember our earlier discussion of the confrontation of Aaron and Miriam against Moses because of his selection for a wife? I know this example is not of a husband and wife. But it gives such a good example of how not to communicate.

The first key in communication is to stick to the subject. Remember that Aaron and Miriam started out talking about

Moses' wife, but before they knew it, they jumped to questioning his authority and whether God spoke only to him. If God had allowed them to continue, we don't know how far they would have gone. And note that these were not Moses' enemies; these were his friends family, as a matter of fact, causing dissension and division. But God dealt with them. So we must use this example to understand that even when something is done that could appear or seem wrong in our eyes or even out of the will of God, we still must be careful what we say because the devil is looking for a way to plant dissension, doubt, and division.

Let's read the text together. Numbers 12:1–16 says:

> *And Miriam and Aaron spake against Moses because of the Ethiopian woman whom he had married: for he had married an Ethiopian woman. And they said, Hath the LORD indeed spoken only by Moses? hath he not spoken also by us? And the LORD heard it. (Now the man Moses was very meek, above all the men which were upon the face of the earth.)*
>
> *And the LORD spake suddenly unto Moses, and unto Aaron, and unto Miriam, Come out ye three unto the tabernacle of the congregation. And they three came out. And the LORD came down in the pillar of the cloud, and stood in the door of the tabernacle, and called Aaron and Miriam: and they both came forth. And he said, Hear now my words: If there be a prophet among you, I the LORD will make myself known unto him in a vision, and will speak unto him in a dream. My servant Moses is not so, who is faithful in all mine house. With him will I speak mouth to mouth, even apparently, and not in dark speeches; and the similitude of the LORD shall he behold: wherefore then were ye not afraid to speak*

against my servant Moses? And the anger of the LORD was kindled against them; and he departed.

And the cloud departed from off the tabernacle; and, behold, Miriam became leprous, white as snow: and Aaron looked upon Miriam, and, behold, she was leprous. And Aaron said unto Moses, Alas, my lord, I beseech thee, lay not the sin upon us, wherein we have done foolishly, and wherein we have sinned. Let her not be as one dead, of whom the flesh is half consumed when he cometh out of his mother's womb. And Moses cried unto the LORD, saying, Heal her now, O God, I beseech thee. And the LORD said unto Moses, If her father had but spit in her face, should she not be ashamed seven days? let her be shut out from the camp seven days, and after that let her be received in again. And Miriam was shut out from the camp seven days: and the people journeyed not till Miriam was brought in again. And afterward the people removed from Hazeroth, and pitched in the wilderness of Paran.

We must always try to deal with the issue at hand, not use the opportunity to speak against someone's character. Our husbands are men of God; we must respect God's order.

Another point we need to make is that Miriam's actions also caused the children of Israel to be held up for seven additional days while God dealt with her. This should be a lesson to us. When we are questioning our husbands, we must make sure God is pleased with our actions. We do not want it to be that our entire house has to stand still and wait, not being able to move forward because God is dealing with us.

Another excellent biblical example of communication and presentation, which resulted in the saving of a nation of people, is the story of Queen Esther. Queen Esther knew presentation was key when going to see the king. We know from the biblical account that Esther was the queen positioned by God. She knew what must be done. But still Esther knew it was important to prepare.

The queen prepared for three days before she ever presented herself to the king. Her preparation may seem to be only physical, but I believe it was more. Queen Esther knew that the nation of Israel was in danger and that her action could make the difference. We should also prepare before talking to our husbands.

The story of Esther begins for me long before she became queen. The story really begins with a queen named Vashti. In the first chapter of Esther, Queen Vashti decided to disobey an order of her husband, King Ahasuerus. The king, because of his concern for his kingdom and the resulting behavior of the wives in his kingdom, had to banish the queen.

The text reads in Esther 1:10–12: *"On the seventh day, when the heart of the king was merry with wine, he commanded Mehuman, Biztha, Harbona, Bigtha, and Abagtha, Zethar, and Carcas, the seven chamberlains that served in the presence of Ahasuerus the king, To bring Vashti the queen before the king with the crown royal, to show the people and the princes her beauty: for she was fair to look on. But the queen Vashti refused to come at the king's commandment by his chamberlains: therefore was the king very wroth, and his anger burned in him."*

Esther 1:17–22 continues:

For this deed of the queen shall come abroad unto all women, so that they shall despise their husbands in their eyes, when it shall be reported, The king Ahasuerus commanded Vashti the queen to be brought in before him, but she came not. Likewise shall the ladies of Persia and Media say this day unto all the king's princes, which have heard of the deed

*of the queen. Thus shall there arise too much con-
tempt and wrath. If it please the king, let there go a
royal commandment from him, and let it be written
among the laws of the Persians and the Medes, that
it be not altered, That Vashti come no more before
king Ahasuerus; and let the king give her royal estate
unto another that is better than she. And when the
king's decree which he shall make shall be published throughout all his empire, (for it is great,) all
the wives shall give to their husbands honour, both
to great and small. And the saying pleased the king
and the princes; and the king did according to the
word of Memucan: For he sent letters into all the
king's provinces, into every province according to
the writing thereof, and to every people after their
language, that every man should bear rule in his own
house, and that it should be published according to
the language of every people.*

We need to remember that all our actions, positive or
negative, affect someone else. Sometimes the impact is far
greater than just its impact on us. So presentation is key.
Maybe Queen Vashti did not come before the king for a
reason only she knew, but her decision was not presented to
him in the best way. In all things, even if we have an important point to make, we should be careful not to disrespect
our husbands in the presence of others, especially if our husbands are in a position of leadership. It will ultimately look
bad on our part.

For Vashti, not to come when her husband requested her
presence was both disrespectful and an open disregard for
the consequence to his command and authority as king. The
concern of the king was that his wife's behavior might be
looked upon as an example to the women within his kingdom
and neighboring kingdoms. Other women might begin to

despise their husbands and follow Vashti's example in their marriages. When you dishonor your husband, someone is always watching. Don't let another sister fall because of your example.

Now let us continue with Esther. After the king banished Vashti, Esther was later named queen. *"So Esther was taken unto king Ahasuerus into his house royal in the tenth month, which is the month Tebeth, in the seventh year of his reign. And the king loved Esther above all the women, and she obtained grace and favour in his sight more than all the virgins; so that he set the royal crown upon her head, and made her queen instead of Vashti"* (Est. 2:16–17). Vashti's loss was Esther's gain.

Esther's first recorded presentation to the king was to tell him of an assassination plot against him. Her uncle Mordecai had knowledge of this plot and the men responsible. But this woman did not hoard all the honor. Esther was quick to tell the king that it was because of her uncle. This would later help her and the children of Israel. *"In those days, while Mordecai sat in the king's gate, two of the king's chamberlains, Bigthan and Teresh, of those which kept the door, were wroth, and sought to lay hand on the king Ahasuerus. And the thing was known to Mordecai, who told it unto Esther the queen; and Esther certified the king thereof in Mordecai's name. And when inquisition was made of the matter, it was found out; therefore they were both hanged on a tree: and it was written in the book of the chronicles before the king"* (Est. 2:21–23).

Esther was already queen, the king loved her, and she already had favour in the king's sight. The fact that she was also an intelligent woman able to move among the people of his kingdom and gather valuable information for the aid of the king must have made Ahasuerus very happy. Ahasuerus reign and kingdom were blessed because of Esther. Again, an example of a husband receiving favour because of his wife (Proverbs 18:22).

The story continues with the introduction of Haman, who had been set by the king to be above all the princes. Haman, because of selfish, prideful reasons, plotted to have Mordecai and all the Jews killed (Est. 3:2–13). Mordecai heard of the plot and enlisted the aid of Queen Esther to come to the defense of the Jewish people. But Esther, being a wise woman, began to prepare herself to see the king on behalf of her people, the Jewish nation.

Esther 4:1-17 records:

> *When Mordecai perceived all that was done, Mordecai rent his clothes, and put on sackcloth with ashes, and went out into the midst of the city, and cried with a loud and a bitter cry; And came even before the king's gate: for none might enter into the king's gate clothed with sackcloth. And in every province, whithersoever the king's commandment and his decree came, there was great mourning among the Jews, and fasting, and weeping, and wailing; and many lay in sackcloth and ashes. So Esther's maids and her chamberlains came and told it her. Then was the queen exceedingly grieved; and she sent raiment to clothe Mordecai, and to take away his sackcloth from him: but he received it not.*
>
> *Then called Esther for Hatach, one of the king's chamberlains, whom he had appointed to attend upon her, and gave him a commandment to Mordecai, to know what it was, and why it was. So Hatach went forth to Mordecai unto the street of the city, which was before the king's gate. And Mordecai told him of all that had happened unto him, and of the sum of the money that Haman had promised to pay to the king's treasuries for the Jews, to destroy them. Also*

he gave him the copy of the writing of the decree that was given at Shushan to destroy them, to show it unto Esther, and to declare it unto her, and to charge her that she should go in unto the king, to make supplication unto him, and to make request before him for her people. And Hatach came and told Esther the words of Mordecai.

Again Esther spake unto Hatach, and gave him commandment unto Mordecai. All the king's servants, and the people of the king's provinces, do know, that whosoever, whether man or woman, shall come unto the king into the inner court, who is not called, there is one law of his to put him to death, except such to whom the king shall hold out the golden sceptre, that he may live: but I have not been called to come in unto the king these thirty days. And they told to Mordecai Esther's words. Then Mordecai commanded to answer Esther, Think not with thyself that thou shalt escape in the king's house, more than all the Jews. For if thou altogether holdest thy peace at this time, then shall there enlargement and deliverance arise to the Jews from another place; but thou and thy father's house shall be destroyed: and who knoweth whether thou art come to the kingdom for such a time as this?

Then Esther bade them return Mordecai this answer, Go, gather together all the Jews that are present in Shushan, and fast ye for me, and neither eat nor drink three days, night or day: I also and my maidens will fast likewise; and so will I go in unto the king, which is not according to the law: and if I perish, I perish. So Mordecai went his way, and did according to all that Esther had commanded him.

Esther knew she must speak to her husband, the king. She had no choice. At this point, the king was the only one who could save her people. But how could she make sure he saw her point of view and decided to save the Jews? The reality was that Haman's craftiness had already convinced the king to get rid of her people, who did not keep the king's laws. It is recorded in Esther 3:8–11:

And Haman said unto king Ahasuerus, There is a certain people scattered abroad and dispersed among the people in all the provinces of thy kingdom; and their laws are diverse from all people; neither keep they the king's laws: therefore it is not for the king's profit to suffer them. If it please the king, let it be written that they may be destroyed: and I will pay ten thousand talents of silver to the hands of those that have the charge of the business, to bring it into the king's treasuries. And the king took his ring from his hand, and gave it unto Haman the son of Hammedatha the Agagite, the Jews' enemy. And the king said unto Haman, The silver is given to thee, the people also, to do with them as it seemeth good to thee.

The truth is, the king had already given permission to kill the Jews. So Esther had to be careful, because the last thing she wanted to say was, "You are wrong," or "You were so easily tricked." Esther knew she must speak to her husband. She must be heard because a nation depended on her. There was no debate that she was right. The only dilemma was when should she speak and how should she present it so she would be heard. Remember, a nation was depending on her presentation.

Esther began to prepare by asking her people to fast with her, and she began to prepare in three days to go to the king. On the third day, she did not go into his inner court with just anything on, but she carefully prepared her body. She adorned herself with royal apparel. She was both spiritually and physically prepared before she opened her mouth. This is a lesson for all of us. It is all in the presentation.

Reading on, Esther 5:1–8 continues:

Now it came to pass on the third day, that Esther put on her royal apparel, and stood in the inner court of the king's house, over against the king's house: and the king sat upon his royal throne in the royal house, over against the gate of the house. And it was so, when the king saw Esther the queen standing in the court, that she obtained favour in his sight: and the king held out to Esther the golden sceptre that was in his hand. So Esther drew near, and touched the top of the sceptre. Then said the king unto her, What wilt thou, queen Esther? and what is thy request? it shall be even given thee to the half of the kingdom. And Esther answered, If it seem good unto the king, let the king and Haman come this day unto the banquet that I have prepared for him. Then the king said, Cause Haman to make haste, that he may do as Esther hath said. So the king and Haman came to the banquet that Esther had prepared.

And the king said unto Esther at the banquet of wine, What is thy petition? and it shall be granted thee: and what is thy request? even to the half of the kingdom it shall be performed. Then answered Esther, and said, My petition and my request is; If I have found favour in the sight of the king, and if it please the king to grant my petition, and to perform my request, let the king and Haman come to the ban-quet that I shall prepare for them, and I will do to morrow as the king hath said.

Let me interject a side note. I am not telling any of us to use tools of manipulation or to try to deceive our husbands. What I am trying to get us all to see is there is a way to approach our husbands and get our points of view heard. Honestly, a good wife should always want to find favor in her husband's sight, and she should strive to always do things in her marriage that make her marriage better. She should seek to please her husband, and he should seek to please her.

For example, don't cook your husband a nice dinner just because you want him to give you something; that is manipulation. If your husband comes home and you look wonderful, the home is cleaned and his favorite meal is waiting on the stove, or you have just bathed and are waiting in a new negligee, and the first thing he says is, "What do you want now?" you know you have a problem. You may have been operating under a spirit of manipulation. But I encourage you to carefully choose the circumstances in which you tell him something. Let's agree to bind any spirit of manipulation operating in our lives—now! With the spirit of manipulation crushed in all our lives, let us continue.

On with the story, and we see that Esther found favor in the sight of the king and invited him to a second dinner. She was a wise woman. I believe the fasting of the people for three days touched God, and He now aided her by dealing with the king. The night following the banquet, the king could not sleep. God used this night to remind Ahasuerus of Mordecai's loyal acts. God brought honor to Mordecai, a Jew, even while the enemy, Haman, built the gallows.

Esther 6:1–3 says, "On that night could not the king sleep, and he commanded to bring the book of records of the chronicles; and they were read before the king. And it was found written, that Mordecai had told of Bigthana and Teresh, two of the king's chamberlains, the keepers of the door, who sought to lay hand on the king Ahasuerus. And the king said, What honour and dignity hath been done to

Mordecai for this? Then said the king's servants that ministered unto him, There is nothing done for him."

With God having set up the Jews, Esther's second banquet gave her an opportunity to present her case. Surely the
king would hear her. Esther 7:1–4 reads:

*So the king and Haman came to banquet with Esther
the queen. And the king said again unto Esther on
the second day at the banquet of wine, What is thy
petition, queen Esther? and it shall be granted thee:
and what is thy request? and it shall be performed,
even to the half of the kingdom. Then Esther the
queen answered and said, If I have found favour in
thy sight, O king, and if it please the king, let my
life be given me at my petition, and my people at
my request: For we are sold, I and my people, to be
destroyed, to be slain, and to perish. But if we had
been sold for bondmen and bondwomen, I had held
my tongue, although the enemy could not countervail
the king's damage.*

Esther's words were prepared and carefully chosen. She
had prepared herself, her home, and her words. We know
the end of the story. The king heard his wife and came to the
defense of her and her people.

Esther 7:5–10 records the story:

*Then the king Ahasuerus answered and said unto
Esther the queen, Who is he, and where is he, that
durst presume in his heart to do so? And Esther said,
The adversary and enemy is this wicked Haman. Then
Haman was afraid before the king and the queen.*

*And the king arising from the banquet of wine in
his wrath went into the palace garden: and Haman
stood up to make request for his life to Esther the*

queen; for he saw that there was evil determined against him by the king. Then the king returned out of the palace garden into the place of the banquet of wine; and Haman was fallen upon the bed whereon Esther was. Then said the king, Will he force the queen also before me in the house? As the word went out of the king's mouth, they covered Haman's face. And Harbonah, one of the chamberlains, said before the king, Behold also, the gallows fifty cubits high, which Haman had made for Mordecai, who had spoken good for the king, standeth in the house of Haman. Then the king said, Hang him thereon. So they hanged Haman on the gallows that he had prepared for Mordecai. Then was the king's wrath pacified.

Esther's presentation saved the nation of Israel. I am not saying that each time we speak to our husbands we must prepare a banquet. But let us be mindful of what we say, how we say it, and where we say it. Remember, there is a time and place for all things.

Our next example of presentation is found in the book of Judges. Although this example is not between a husband and wife, it is an another excellent example of communication and support. The prophetess Deborah was a wife and a judge of Israel. God had raised her up to judge all of Israel. With this call on her life, she could have become bossy and overbearing because of who she was, but she shows us that presentation in every aspect of life, marriage, and ministry is important.

Judges 4:4–5 says, *"And Deborah, a prophetess, the wife of Lapidoth, she judged Israel at that time. And she dwelt under the palm tree of Deborah between Ramah and Bethel in mount Ephraim: and the children of Israel came up to her for judgment."*

Deborah, a prophetess and a judge, had to speak with Barak concerning his disobedience, and at the same time, she had to encourage him not to be afraid and to go forward in the victory God had already given him against Sisera, the captain of Jabin's army. Judges 4:6–10 reads:

And she sent and called Barak the son of Abinoam out of Kedeshnaphtali, and said unto him, Hath not the LORD God of Israel commanded, saying, Go and draw toward mount Tabor, and take with the e ten thousand men of the children of Naphtali and of the children of Zebulun? And I will draw unto thee to the river Kishon Sisera, the captain of Jabin's army, with his chariots and his multitude; and I will deliver him into thine hand. And Barak said unto her, If thou wilt go with me, then I will go: but if thou wilt not go with me, then I will not go. And she said, I will surely go with thee: notwithstanding the journey that thou takest shall not be for thine honour; for the LORD shall sell Sisera into the hand of a woman. And Deborah arose, and went with Barak to Kedesh. And Barak called Zebulun and Naphtali to Kedesh; and he went up with ten thousand men at his feet: and Deborah went up with him.

Deborah encouraged Barak with her words and her deeds. She was ready to go with him, even if it meant going to battle, because she was sure of God's words herself. It will be hard for us as wives to encourage our husbands or provoke them to heed to the word of the Lord if we don't believe His word ourselves.

Judges 4:14–16 says:

And Deborah said unto Barak, Up; for this is the day in which the LORD hath delivered Sisera into thine hand: is not the LORD gone out before thee? So Barak went down from mount Tabor, and ten thousand men after him. And the LORD discomfited Sisera, and all his chariots, and all his host, with the edge of the sword before Barak; so that Sisera lighted down off his chariot, and fled away on his feet. But Barak pursued after the chariots, and after the host, unto Harosheth of the Gentiles: and all the host of Sisera fell upon the edge of the sword; and there was not a man left.

In the end, God confused the enemy and gave the children of Israel the victory. But what if Deborah had approached Barak with an attitude? Imagine her, with her hands on her hips and a giant attitude, coming to tell him how wrong he was, telling him that he was a coward and could not hear God, telling him he was disobedient and she had to tell him everything. Where would Barak have gone? We definitely know he would not have asked Deborah to go with him.

Presentation is everything, so let all your actions and reactions be appropriate for the situation. Let God teach you how to talk to your husband. It is not enough to be right if no one hears you. So be focused, deal with the issue, and be wise in your presentation.

Chapter 7

Presentation Is Everything

Chapter Prayer

God, I know that I am the anointed helpmeet.
And God, just as You have taught me what to give
my husband,
help me to learn how to give it to him.

God, even when I am right,
help me to present my views to my husband in the
right way.
I do not want to be a manipulative woman.
Neither do I want to rely on deceit and craftiness
in my communications with my husband.

I do not want hidden motives when I approach
my husband.
But God, help me to talk to him with a pure heart,
and let my only motive be to please You
by helping my husband.
God, even if my husband is wrong,
allow me to present my view in a loving and
uplifting way.
God, continue to teach me
how to approach, listen and speak my husband.
Amen.

Chapter 8

A Season for All Things
ରୀ(ଡ

Ecclesiastes 3:11: *"He hath made every thing beautiful in his time."*

Let's get something straight right now, and we'll keep it between us girls: Wonder Woman is a cartoon character. And guess what? So is Batgirl, Superwoman, and all the other "she" heroes. Furthermore, none of them ever had a husband, children, home, job, ministry, or extended family. If they had, I am positive they would not have been flying around so much!

Living today in this society, we are tricked into believing that if we don't do it all and have it all, we are less than or not enough. The lie is thinking we don't have a full life unless our lives are overfilled. The world has told us to be loving, nurturing, caring wives, always at our husbands' sides. We are told to be encouragers and supporters; with perfect makeup and impeccable dress. We should also be attentive mothers, always anticipating our children's every need, physically, emotionally, and academically. On top of that, our Christian walk tells us to be a help to friends and family. We are also told to be career women excelling in corporate America, and of course, we should never take a sick day for us or the children, never miss a deadline, and never be late, no matter what happened on the way to school. We are to also have a God-directed, saint-delivering, devil-destroying ministry that stretches the length and breadth of this country; oh, and only in churches that will allow women to minister. We are to do all this and still wear a size 6. Hm-m-m . . .

But thank God for His word in Ecclesiastes, because we know that life has seasons. We don't have to do everything today. We don't have to live by today's standards. Let's look at God's word concerning seasons.

Ecclesiastes 3:1–8, 11 says:

> *To every thing there is a season, and a time to every purpose under the heaven: A time to be born, and a time to die; a time to plant, and a time to pluck up that which is planted; A time to kill, and a time to heal; a time to break down, and a time to build up; A time to weep, and a time to laugh; a time to mourn, and a time to dance; A time to cast away stones, and a time to gather stones together; a time to embrace, and a time to refrain from embracing; A time to get, and a time to lose; a time to keep, and a time to cast away; A time to rend, and a time to sew; a time to keep silence, and a time to speak; A time to love, and a time to hate; a time of war, and a time of peace. . . . He hath made every thing beautiful in his time.*

After reading our text, I just want to encourage you to slow down and take inventory of what is going on in your life. And the question I want you to answer is, where are you? What season are you in? Is your life filled with so many tasks that you are not living but just performing one task after another?

I asked myself recently what were the things in my life that I had decided to do that were really not necessary. Was

I on my schedule or God's schedule? I was at a point in my life that I had so much to do that I did not even want to get out of bed in the morning. And God showed me a lot of what I was doing was started by me because I had convinced myself, with the influence of the world, that this is where I should be, or this is what I should be doing, or this is what the children should be doing, or this is what my husband should be doing.

Then God took me to Jeremiah 29:11: *"For I know the thoughts that I think toward you, saith the LORD, thoughts of peace, and not of evil, to give you an expected end."* This Scripture blessed me so much. It freed me from every man-made expectation, even some of my own self-imposed stress givers. See, what God has for you, only He knows. He knows every plan and season. So stop trying in your flesh to do and to be everything. God is not asking you to be all things. He is asking you to seek Him, listen for His voice, and then be obedient and follow His direction. Hm-m-m . . . it sounds kind of simple stated that way!

But to get to the simple, we have to change the way we think about so many things. We have got to trust God for our entire lives and know that the seasons have been directed by Him. If we confess Jesus as Lord and Savior, confess that God is Alpha and Omega, and believe that God orders our steps, then surely we must realize that He knows each step we must take and each season we must travel though. We must rest in God, who knows the plans for our lives. The most important word in Jeremiah 29:11 is end. He already knows were He wants you to end, where he expects you to end, so trust Him.

One particular issue I want us to discuss is the decision to work in or out of the home. I believe this is a very personal choice, and no one should tell another woman her choice is wrong or try to impose a personal view concerning that woman's choice. I do not believe there is a definite right or a

definite wrong answer, but I think each of us should pray and
ask God to tell us our season. I believe if we seek Him and
pray to be in His will, enjoying the place He has us today, He
will bless each season of life. Let's look now at an example
of a woman used while at home.

The account of Jael in the book of Judges is a great
example of a woman, a wife, being just where God could
use her. Let's read the account in Judges 4:15–24:

> And the LORD discomfited Sisera, and all his
> chariots, and all his host, with the edge of the sword
> before Barak; so that Sisera lighted down off his
> chariot, and fled away on his feet. But Barak pursued
> after the chariots, and after the host, unto Harosheth
> of the Gentiles: and all the host of Sisera fell upon
> the edge of the sword; and there was not a man left.
>
> Howbeit Sisera fled away on his feet to the tent of
> Jael the wife of Heber the Kenite: for there was peace
> between Jabin the king of Hazor and the house of
> Heber the Kenite. And Jael went out to meet Sisera,
> and said unto him, Turn in, my lord, turn in to me;
> fear not. And when he had turned in unto her into the
> tent, she covered him with a mantle. And he said unto
> her, Give me, I pray thee, a little water to drink; for I
> am thirsty. And she opened a bottle of milk, and gave
> him drink, and covered him. Again he said unto her,
> Stand in the door of the tent, and it shall be, when
> any man doth come and enquire of thee, and say, Is
> there any man here? that thou shalt say, No. Then
> Jael Heber's wife took a nail of the tent, and took
> an hammer in her hand, and went softly unto him,
> and smote the nail into his temples, and fastened it
> into the ground: for he was fast asleep and weary.
> So he died. And, behold, as Barak pursued Sisera,
> Jael came out to meet him, and said unto him, Come,

*and I will show thee the man whom thou seekest.
And when he came into her tent, behold, Sisera lay
dead, and the nail was in his temples. So God sub-
dued on that day Jabin the king of Canaan before
the children of Israel. And the hand of the children
of Israel prospered, and prevailed against Jabin the
king of Canaan, until they had destroyed Jabin king
of Canaan.*

Jael was in the desert, maybe all alone, maybe surrounded
by her servants and children. The Bible does not say exactly,
but she was just where God needed her to be. His reward to
Jael was honor.

Don't worry about staying at home. Maybe you want to
put your career on hold. Jael, while staying at home where
God had her, was still in her season. Jael was used by God,
and her name is celebrated.

Now, we all won't be able to stay home, but the key here
is, where does God want you today? Where does He want
you for this season? You see, Deborah, the prophetess, did
not stay home, but she too was in the will of God. Prophetess
Deborah went with Barak to fight, while Jael was home in
her tent (Judg. 4:11).

You see, it was all a part of God's plan for Jael. God
had already spoken in Judges 4:9 that a woman (Jael) would
receive honor: *"And she said, I will surely go with thee: notwithstanding the journey that thou takest shall not be for
thine honour; for the LORD shall sell Sisera into the hand of
a woman."* As Deborah stated she would go into battle with
Barack, she also explained who would get the honor from
the battle. But what if Jael had awakened that morning and
decided to be somewhere else—you know, did not want to
be in the tent?

So sisters, I encourage you to know the season of your
life, and do not be jealous of someone else's season. You

never know what a person has had to go through in order to get to each season. Not only should you know the season you are in, but you should also delight and have joy in that season.

There is a resting place in God. I never understood the meaning of rest in God until I learned how to totally trust Him. So don't worry about not having this particular thing, or being a certain age and not having done a certain task or reached a certain accomplishment in life. But totally give your life to Him, and accept each plan He has for you as being the right plan. It is not a race to go the farthest or have the most.

Measure yourself only by the Word of God. Pray for God's confirmation about where you should be and what you should be doing. Quiet the voices that would compare you to others. This is not a rat race. This is your life. You may not travel the world now. Your ministry may have slowed down because you have chosen to work on your marriage, or you may have just had a baby or have teenagers who need their mother at home. But seek God for your season, and know that His timing is perfect.

The race should be to the place God has for you and only you, and find your joy in each season. Learn how to be thankful no matter where you may be, because God knows the plan. As Philippians 4:12 reads, *"I know both how to be abased, and I know how to abound: every where and in all things I am instructed both to be full and to be hungry, both to abound and to suffer need."* Remember God knows your expected end. Trust God to get you there.

Chapter 8

A Season for All Things

Chapter Prayer

God thank you for my Expected End.
I am a unique individual and my seasons are
set by You.
God, help me to know my season and delight in it!
God, help me to trust You totally and to rest in Your
plans for my life.

God, I thank You for loving me so much that You
have made plans just for me.
Help me not to judge myself or measure my
accomplishments against someone else's.
I need only to trust in Your plans for my life.
God, help me when I would get frustrated or panic
or be afraid.
You will make the seasons of my life beautiful in
Your time.
Help me to see the beauty in each season and to
celebrate each season.
With thanks I await each season, to my expected end.
In Jesus' name,
Amen.

Chapter 9

Protector of the Anointing
๑\๏

Again, I am in awe of God. Everything that God did concerning the creation of the woman was meaningful, down to where he took her from. Eve was made from the rib (side) of Adam. Genesis 2:21–22 says, *"And the LORD God caused a deep sleep to fall upon Adam, and he slept: and he took one of his ribs, and closed up the flesh instead thereof; And the rib, which the LORD God had taken from man, made he a woman, and brought her unto the man."* In this chapter, we are going to explore how important a rib is to the body and how this translates to the spiritual connection between a husband and his wife.

The significance of a rib or the rib cage is one of protection. The twenty-four thin, flat, curved bones make up twelve pairs of ribs, which are joined together to form the rib cage. The rib cage protects the organs of the body. The ribs protect the heart, lungs, and other parts of the body from injury or shock that might damage them. The ribs also protect parts of the stomach, spleen, and kidneys. The ribs also help us to breathe while giving the chest its shape. The ribs have also been made to be flexible and springy; this enables them to absorb a force without the force hurting the organs. A rib is sometimes broken when protecting the organ. The design of each is rib is in order to accomplish its purpose. These purposes, although natural, mimic the spiritual and the emotional purposes that we as wives should have in our relationships with our husbands.

All these natural characteristics of the ribs and rib cage speak to and are so integral to our spiritual purpose as wives. We as women are strong yet flexible. We are versatile and springy, able to bounce back. We support, protect, and help in giving shape. All this, yet we are fragile and may be broken in order to protect. We aid in the protection of the vital places of our men, just as the natural ribs help in the protection of the vital organs of the body. I like to call these vital places in our husbands their soft spots.

The one soft spot that I want to talk about is the heart. Just as the ribs protect vital spots in the natural, I believe the wife helps protect them in the spiritual realm. I want to cor-relate this in the spiritual, if you would allow me to explain. We know that the heart is the organ that pumps blood to all the needed areas of the body and that the blood carries oxygen to the organs. A heart that is weakened, wounded, overworked, under pressure, under appreciated, neglected, and even sometimes abused may not function effectively.

You see, the heart is a muscle; it takes in blood and pumps blood out. The heart's ability to supply blood and therefore oxygen to the body has a direct correlation on the body's ability to function. A damaged heart yields a low blood supply and low oxygen and causes the body to function from a place of weakness. However, a heart that is strong is able to supply the correct quantities of blood and oxygen. The body then functions from a position of strength and can accom-plish its purpose.

So what does this have to do with you and your husband? I would like to suggest to you that just as there is a natural heart that supplies the natural man, there is also a spiritual heart where a person keeps his or her innermost thoughts and dreams. It is the place from which we encourage ourselves.

Let's go further. What if the physical heart is so damaged it cannot take in blood, the life source of each body? We may ask the same question if the heart cannot pump blood or deliver blood to the organs. In that case, the body will not survive for very long. This organ, the heart, is protected from damage by the ribs. The heart must function for the body to function; any impact has to penetrate the ribs before it can get to the heart. Remember, in the beginning, you were created from a rib.

So how does the spiritual rib protect the spiritual heart? The spiritual heart of a man is one soft spot in particular that must operate effectively and must be protected in order for his spiritual life to continue. Just as I am not talking about a physical rib of protection, I am also not talking about the physical heart. I must clarify this heart. The heart I am speaking about is the intangible place where we store our secrets, dreams, wishes, desires, hurts, pains, fears, plans, and unspoken promises. It is the place from which we hope.

You cannot reach just anyone's heart by some brief, casual acquaintance. Only after your husband has uncovered himself to you and allowed you in are you able to see his soft spot, his heart. You should not take this vulnerability casually, but instead you should guard it with the instinct of a lioness. Your husband's heart should receive only protection from you. It should never be in danger from you.

The Bible calls the heart that with which we love, seek, and serve God. Deuteronomy 4:29 says, *"But if from thence thou shalt seek the LORD thy God, thou shalt find him, if thou seek him with all thy heart and with all thy soul."*

The heart is also where we fear God and keep His commandments. Deuteronomy 5:29 says, *"O that there were such an heart in them, that they would fear me, and keep all my commandments always, that it might be well with them, and with their children for ever!"*

The heart is where we put the Word of God. The heart is where we name our enemies and name ourselves. Deuteronomy 7:17 records, *"If thou shalt say in thine heart, These nations are more than I; how can I dispossess them?"*

The vision of ministry is kept in the heart. 2 Samuel 7:3 reads, *"And Nathan said to the king, Go, do all that is in thine heart; for the LORD is with thee"*; and in 1 Chronicles 28:2, the Bible reads, *"Then David the king stood up upon his feet, and said, Hear me, my brethren, and my people: As for me, I had in mine heart to build an house of rest for the ark of the covenant of the LORD, and for the footstool of our God, and had made ready for the building."*

Our hearts are gifts from God to keep His commandments, testimonies, and statutes. 1 Chronicles 29:19 says, *"And give unto Solomon my son a perfect heart, to keep thy commandments, thy testimonies, and thy statutes, and to do all these things, and to build the palace, for the which I have made provision."* The Scriptures continue in regards to the heart.

So much is tied into a man's heart. Have you ever been with your husband when he begins to talk vision for the family, the ministry, a business venture, or the community? He begins to stare off from you as if he has left you. But he has not left you; it is just that God is showing him so much at that moment, and he begins to unveil and explain to you all that he sees, all that is in his heart to do. He tells you what he sees God doing through him, what he thinks can happen. He has just let you in to see his soft spot.

At that moment, what do you say? Do you agree? Are you excited? Do you encourage? Because the truth is, he just showed you his soft spot; he just uncovered what was in his heart. How will you protect it now and later?

The Word of God says in Proverbs 31:11–12, *"The heart of her husband doth safely trust in her, so that he shall have no need of spoil. She will do him good and not evil all the days of her life."* Can you be trusted with your husband's heart? This should not be a question the anointed helpmeet should even think about. The answer must be yes. If we are to walk with our husbands as God leads them through life, through each season, some good and some not so good, they must be able to trust us. God helps us to be the wives our husbands' hearts can be safely entrusted to.

Let's talk about some examples of a damaged heart and explore how we can stop hurting our husbands' hearts and stop others from hurting them. For example, a wounded heart may become bitter, or as a defense mechanism, the heart may shut out others and become hardened and cold. A disappointed heart may become heavy or depressed. The disappointments may cause the heart to stop dreaming. But a heart that is encouraged and supported will be more likely to step out.

Please do not misunderstand me. I don't believe you can or should control your husband's heart, nor do I believe that his heart is your responsibility. I believe that each of us must give an account of what is in our hearts. Only God knows the hearts of men; after all, He holds the heart of the king. But I do believe God has placed us to speak life into the hearts of our husbands.

Although the Bible says God strengthens the heart, the wife also plays a role as recorded in Scripture to the turning of a man's heart, and she is often privy to the contents of his heart. Let's explore how we can help, hinder, or prayerfully protect our husbands' soft spots, their hearts.

Betrayal is often the most wounding and detrimental thing to the heart. We must be careful not to hurt our husbands with betrayal when they tell us what is in their hearts. Judges 16:17-18 says of Samson:

"He told her all his heart, and said unto her, There hath not come a razor upon mine head; for I have been a Nazarite unto God from my mother's womb: if I be shaven, then my strength will go from me, and I shall become weak, and be like any other man.

And when Delilah saw that he had told her all his heart, she sent and called for the lords of the Philistines, saying, Come up this once, for he hath showed me all his heart. Then the lords of the Philistines came up unto her, and brought money in their hand."

In the text, Delilah was told all that was in Samson's heart. Instead of thanking God for their closeness, or thanking God that Samson could trust her with all his closest truths, or feeling honored that he allowed her to see his heart, she betrayed him with the contents of his heart and used it against him. Her actions ended up destroying Samson.

We as wives also have a great influence in our husbands' lives. We also want to be careful what we pour into our husbands' hearts and what we turn their hearts to. Solomon is known as the wisest man ever, yet his heart was turned from God by his wives. What does this say about the power of a woman to influence her husband?

1Kings 11:4 says, *"For it came to pass, when Solomon was old, that his wives turned away his heart after other gods: and his heart was not perfect with the LORD his God, as was the heart of David his father."* In Deuteronomy 11:16, we read, *"Take heed to yourselves, that your heart be not deceived, and ye turn aside, and serve other gods, and worship them."* God is a jealous God, and He will have no other gods before Him. He warns us in these two Scriptures not to serve other gods.

But look at what happened to Solomon in his old age at the hands of his wives. Now this was King Solomon, who had been given wisdom from God to rule over God's people. What happened here is it that his wives turned his heart from God. We, the anointed helpmeets, never want this charge on our lives.

I am going to talk about a touchy subject here that I am sure will hit a little close to home for all the wives that love their husbands. As we protect and influence their hearts, let's not hold back from encouraging them because we fear their destinies may take them away from us. Let me clarify my statement; the truth is, we want to spend time with our husbands, and we want them to do all God has for them to do, go all the places God as for them to go, and see all the people God has for them to see. We also want them home early every night and want the weekends reserved just for us and the children (for those of us who have them). So how do we balance our relationships with our husbands without pulling at them to the point that we pull them from God?

I was once told, "Don't worry about your husband going so much, because as God elevates him, He will elevate you. And as God promotes him, He will promote you. As his finances increase, your finances increase." My problem with the "Don't worry . . ." answer is that after you find yourself in a big house with two new cars, furniture, and all the fixings, you just want your husband to come through the door and talk to you. You want him next to you in the luxury car, and you want him next to you in the movie theater, and you want him with you in the restaurant. So I had to ask God to help me understand my husband's calling and all God had for him to do. We must not let our desires pull our husbands away from God's desires. Remember, in chapter 6 we discussed the consequences of "because you hearkened to the voice of your wife."

The heart may also be a place of hurt and bitterness, becoming cold and indifferent because of past pain. The heart may harbor unforgiveness, envy, pain, or disappointment. A damaged heart must be rehabilitated or replaced. But God has this covered. In this case, we can encourage, but we need God to repair or give our husbands new hearts.

The rib cage helps give the chest shape. We must support our husbands as God continues to shape and mold them. Many times our mere presence gives them integrity when they stand. Only God could have known all that we as women would need to be. Only God could have known all the roles we would play. Only God could have known we would mimic the roles of the ribs so closely.

The reason why I call us women protectors of the anointing is because the anointing is the power of God on our lives. The anointing on our lives is the manifestation of God's power through our lives as we walk in victory. But what if we have the power of God, the anointing, yet we never tap into it, or maybe we once were powerful but are no longer? The reasons for this may range from low confidence, unbelief, or past pain, but whatever it is, it is stopping us from operating in the power of God in our lives.

You see, when a man's heart has been damaged for whatever reason, the point is, he no longer operates in the full power of God. It seems he has lost the ability to tap into the anointing. I am sure none of us would like to think of our husbands as not being all God has called them to be. Although we cannot keep, care, or cover our husbands, we can always be there to watch and pray for things that can affect their hearts. But I encourage you to be careful in your protecting. Be careful that while protecting, you do not become injured yourself.

In the natural body, an injury to a rib may mean the entire body has to rest or slow down. Pain and some swelling at the particular rib may occur. It will also be painful when taking a deep breath, coughing, or sneezing. Just as the physical body needs a healed rib, so does the spiritual rib need to be healthy. So take care of yourself.

The only treatment for an injury to a rib is rest. In the natural, rest allows the rib to repair itself. The natural healing for a rib may take as much as three to six weeks. If sufficient rest is not given, then the body does not have enough time to heal. I am not telling you that you will definitely be hurt or injured. But I do caution you to care for yourself as well as for your husband.

Chapter 9

Protector of the Anointing

Chapter Prayer

God, Your creation of the woman was so complete
when You created us, even to where You brought us
from in the natural.
Each part of our creation had a meaning.
Thank You, God, for showing us how important
we are in Your plans.

Thank You for showing us how our roles are needed
as we walk with our husbands on the journey You
have laid before us.
Teach us to care for and protect our husbands'
soft spots.
Help us to protect our husbands' vital organs.
Help us to protect their anointing.

God, for all that You do through us,
we will give You all praise and glory.
In the name of Jesus,
Amen.

Chapter 10

Even the Small Things Matter
๑๖

Proverbs 18:21: *"Death and life are in the power of
the tongue: and they that love it shall eat the fruit
thereof."*

Matthew 12:37: *"For by thy words thou shalt
be justified, and by thy words thou shalt be
condemned."*

Well, since we have gone this far, let's keep going.
One quick question: what were the words you spoke
about your husband under your breath when you thought no
one was listening? In this chapter, I want to admonish you
to always encourage your husband in whatever he is doing
in the will of God. Sometimes we don't know all that God
has for him or for ourselves, for that matter. So we must be
careful what we allow to be said and what we allow ourselves to say.

One thing we do know is that Proverbs 18:21 says, *"Life
and death are in the power of the tongue."* The smallest word
or the shortest sentence or phrase can plant a seed of doubt or
disbelief that will grow roots in the spirit and kill a promise
that would have brought forth great harvest. When Moses

sent in twelve spies, only two returned with a good report. The others spoke no good thing, only an evil report. They spoke words of doubt, words that brought forth death rather than life, words that caused fear in the hearts of the children of Israel. The key for us to remember here is they received exactly what they spoke. They even turned the people to their opinion. And it caused an entire nation to wander in the wilderness for an additional forty years.

Let's look at the Bible account in Numbers 13:1–33:

And the LORD spake unto Moses, saying, Send thou men, that they may search the land of Canaan, which I give unto the children of Israel: of every tribe of their fathers shall ye send a man, every one a ruler among them. And Moses by the commandment of the LORD sent them from the wilderness of Paran: all those men were heads of the children of Israel. And these were their names: of the tribe of Reuben, Shammua the son of Zaccur. Of the tribe of Simeon, Shaphat the son of Hori. Of the tribe of Judah, Caleb the son of Jephunneh. Of the tribe of Issachar, Igal the son of Joseph. Of the tribe of Ephraim, Oshea the son of Nun. Of the tribe of Benjamin, Palti the son of Raphu. Of the tribe of Zebulun, Gaddiel the son of Sodi. Of the tribe of Joseph, namely, of the tribe of Manasseh, Gaddi the son of Susi. Of the tribe of Dan, Ammiel the son of Gemalli. Of the tribe of Asher, Sethur the son of Michael. Of the tribe of Naphtali, Nahbi the son of Vophsi. Of the tribe of Gad, Geuel the son of Machi. These are the names of the men which Moses sent to spy out the land. And Moses called Oshea the son of Nun Jehoshua.

And Moses sent them to spy out the land of Canaan, and said unto them, Get you up this way southward, and go up into the mountain: And see the land, what it is; and the people that dwelleth therein, whether they be strong or weak, few or many; And what the land is that they dwell in, whether it be good or bad; and what cities they be that they dwell in, whether in tents, or in strong holds; And what the land is, whether it be fat or lean, whether there be wood therein, or not. And be ye of good courage, and bring of the fruit of the land. Now the time was the time of the first ripe grapes.

So they went up, and searched the land from the wilderness of Zin unto Rehob, as men come to Hamath. And they ascended by the south, and came unto Hebron; where Ahiman, Sheshai, and Talmai, the children of Anak, were. (Now Hebron was built seven years before Zoan in Egypt.) And they came unto the brook of Eshcol, and cut down from thence a branch with one cluster of grapes, and they bare it between two upon a staff; and they brought of the pomegranates, and of the figs. The place was called the brook Eshcol, because of the cluster of grapes which the children of Israel cut down from thence. And they returned from searching of the land after forty days.

And they went and came to Moses, and to Aaron, and to all the congregation of the children of Israel, unto the wilderness of Paran, to Kadesh; and brought back word unto them, and unto all the congregation, and showed them the fruit of the land. And they told him, and said, We came unto the land whither thou sentest us, and surely it floweth with milk and honey; and this is the fruit of it. Nevertheless the people be strong that dwell in the land, and the cities are walled, and very great: and moreover we saw the children of Anak there. The Amalekites dwell in the land of the south: and the Hittites, and the Jebusites, and the

Amorites, dwell in the mountains: and the Canaanites dwell by the sea, and by the coast of Jordan. And Caleb stilled the people before Moses, and said, Let us go up at once, and possess it; for we are well able to overcome it. But the men that went up with him said, We be not able to go up against the people; for they are stronger than we. And they brought up an evil report of the land which they had searched unto the children of Israel, saying, The land, through which we have gone to search it, is a land that eateth up the inhabitants thereof; and all the people that we saw in it are men of a great stature. And there we saw the giants, the sons of Anak, which come of the giants: and we were in our own sight as grasshoppers, and so we were in their sight.

Whenever I read this text, I am always amazed at the disproportionate results. Only two of the twelve believed God would give them the victory. Now think about this: God had told Moses to choose leaders, "rulers among them." So these men were in leadership positions within the children of Israel. But the ten could not see God's plan, and because they could not see or did not understand God, they gave an evil report. Do not be like the ten. Constantly speak a good report. You want to make sure you go into the promised land.

There were consequences for the evil report of the ten. Let's read Number 14:1–39:

"And all the congregation lifted up their voice, and cried; and the people wept that night. And all the children of Israel murmured against Moses and against Aaron: and the whole congregation said unto them, Would God that we had died in the land of Egypt! or would God we had died in this wilderness! And wherefore hath the LORD brought us unto

this land, to fall by the sword, that our wives and our children should be a prey? were it not better for us to return into Egypt? And they said one to another, Let us make a captain, and let us return into Egypt.

Then Moses and Aaron fell on their faces before all the assembly of the congregation of the children of Israel. And Joshua the son of Nun, and Caleb the son of Jephunneh, which were of them that searched the land, rent their clothes: And they spake unto all the company of the children of Israel, saying, The land, which we passed through to search it, is an exceeding good land. If the LORD delight in us, then he will bring us into this land, and give it us; a land which floweth with milk and honey. Only rebel not ye against the LORD, neither fear ye the people of the land; for they are bread for us: their defence is departed from them, and the LORD is with us: fear them not. But all the congregation bade stone them with stones. And the glory of the LORD appeared in the tabernacle of the congregation before all the children of Israel.

And the LORD said unto Moses, How long will this people provoke me? and how long will it be ere they believe me, for all the signs which I have showed among them? I will smite them with the pestilence, and disinherit them, and will make of thee a greater nation and mightier than they.

And Moses said unto the LORD, Then the Egyptians shall hear it, (for thou broughtest up this people in thy might from among them;) And they will tell it to the inhabitants of this land: for they have heard that thou LORD art among this people, that thou LORD art seen face to face, and that thy cloud standeth over them, and that thou goest before them, by day time in a pillar of a cloud, and in a pillar of fire by night.

Now if thou shalt kill all this people as one man, then the nations which have heard the fame of thee will speak, saying, Because the LORD was not able to bring this people into the land which he sware unto them, therefore he hath slain them in the wilderness. And now, I beseech thee, let the power of my Lord be great, according as thou hast spoken, saying, The LORD is longsuffering, and of great mercy, forgiving iniquity and transgression, and by no means clearing the guilty, visiting the iniquity of the fathers upon the children unto the third and fourth generation. Pardon, I beseech thee, the iniquity of this people according unto the greatness of thy mercy, and as thou hast forgiven this people, from Egypt even until now.

And the LORD said, I have pardoned according to thy word: But as truly as I live, all the earth shall be filled with the glory of the LORD. Because all those men which have seen my glory, and my miracles, which I did in Egypt and in the wilderness, and have tempted me now these ten times, and have not hearkened to my voice; Surely they shall not see the land which I sware unto their fathers, neither shall any of them that provoked me see it: But my servant Caleb, because he had another spirit with him, and hath followed me fully, him will I bring into the land whereinto he went; and his seed shall possess it. (Now the Amalekites and the Canaanites dwelt in the valley.) To morrow turn you, and get you into the wilderness by the way of the Red sea.

And the LORD spake unto Moses and unto Aaron, saying, How long shall I bear with this evil congregation, which murmur against me? I have heard the murmurings of the children of Israel, which they murmur against me. Say unto them, As truly as I live, saith the LORD, as ye have spoken in mine ears, so will I do to you: Your carcases shall fall in this wilderness; and all that were numbered of you, according to your whole number, from twenty years old and upward, which have murmured against me, Doubtless ye shall not come into the land, concerning which I sware to make you dwell therein, save Caleb the son of Jephunneh, and Joshua the son of Nun. But your little ones, which ye said should be a prey, them will I bring in, and they shall know the land which ye have despised. But as for you, your carcases, they shall fall in this wilderness. And your children shall wander in the wilderness forty years, and bear your whoredoms, until your carcases be wasted in the wilderness. After the number of the days in which ye searched the land, even forty days, each day for a year, shall ye bear your iniquities, even forty years, and ye shall know my breach of promise. I the LORD have said, I will surely do it unto all this evil congregation, that are gathered together against me: in this wilderness they shall be consumed, and there they shall die.

And the men, which Moses sent to search the land, who returned, and made all the congregation to murmur against him, by bringing up a slander upon the land, Even those men that did bring up the evil report upon the land, died by the plague before the LORD. But Joshua the son of Nun, and Caleb the son of Jephunneh, which were of the men that went to search the land, lived still. And Moses told these sayings unto all the children of Israel: and the people mourned greatly."

As I read in Numbers 14:1–39, I am amazed at the children of Israel. They lifted their voices and cried against Moses and Aaron. They cried to go back to Egypt—back to bondage, back to lack, back to a land that was not promised to them! They murmured against Moses, who had brought them out of Egypt; Moses, who had brought the ten plagues; Moses, who spoke face-to-face with God. Were they not afraid?

But we really cannot judge them. We need to ask if we can see ourselves in this text. Have we raised our voices against God's plan? This might be our least favorite chapter, but let's go all the way in.

It is the words we speak, sometimes even within ourselves. What are the small words you speak in your home concerning your family and your husband? You know, the small one-syllable words and brief phrases like "sure," "we'll see," "whatever," "maybe," "okay," "um-m-m," "right." And don't forget "I guess you can" or "if you say so." Remember, we will give an account for all our words.

The Word of God warns us of the use of even idle words. Matthew 12:36–37 says, "But I say unto you, That every idle word that men shall speak, they shall give account thereof in the day of judgment. For by thy words thou shalt be justified, and by thy words thou shalt be condemned."

Let's take a little self-examination. Has your spouse ever come home and said something or done something you did not fully understand? I mean, you just missed it. What did you do next? What did you say next? Did you say something negative, or did you just sit there with disbelief all over your face? Did you look at him like he was crazy? How encouraging were you at that moment?

I know you have heard this before, but again I say, pray. It is better to just pray for understanding than to speak a word, even a small word, against your husband. Not only can your words discourage and hinder your husband, but they could cause you to miss your promise, your wealthy place. Your words could cause you to wander in the wilderness for some extended time. Your words could cause you not to enter into the promise of God.

This is shown to us in the Scriptures. As Numbers 14:35–37 says, *"I the LORD have said, I will surely do it unto all this evil congregation, that are gathered together against me: in this wilderness they shall be consumed, and there they shall die. And the men, which Moses sent to search the land, who returned, and made all the congregation to murmur against him, by bringing up a slander upon the land, Even those men that did bring up the evil report upon the land, died by the plague before the LORD."*

Let's continue and take a look at a lord, the king's amour bearer, in the Scriptures who did not believe and spoke against the Word of God. We are not judging in this book. But we are using this example to realize that when we doubt what God has spoken to and through our husbands, we are doubting God.

This next text show the consequences of saying even a few small words. I encourage you to read the entire text, 2 Kings 7:1–20, but we will focus on 2 Kings 7:1–2: *"Then Elisha said, Hear ye the word of the LORD; Thus saith the LORD, To morrow about this time shall a measure of fine flour be sold for a shekel, and two measures of barley for a shekel, in the gate of Samaria. Then a lord on whose hand the king leaned answered the man of God, and said, Behold, if the LORD would make windows in heaven, might this thing be? And he said, Behold, thou shalt see it with thine eyes, but shalt not eat thereof."*

We continue with 2 Kings 7:16–20:

So a measure of fine flour was sold for a shekel, and two measures of barley for a shekel, according to the word of the LORD. And the king appointed the lord on whose hand he leaned to have the charge of the gate: and the people trode upon him in the gate, and he

*died, as the man of God had said, who spake when
the king came down to him. And it came to pass as
the man of God had spoken to the king, saying, Two
measures of barley for a shekel, and a measure of
fine flour for a shekel, shall be to morrow about this
time in the gate of Samaria: And that lord answered
the man of God, and said, Now, behold, if the LORD
should make windows in heaven, might such a thing
be? And he said, Behold, thou shalt see it with thine
eyes, but shalt not eat thereof. And so it fell out unto
him: for the people trode upon him in the gate, and
he died.*

Sometimes God wants to do something in our lives, marriages, or ministries that may seem difficult or impossible to us. Or God might be saying He is going to bless us, but because we are focusing on our present situation, we cannot see how He will bring the blessing to pass. We must not question God. We see in 2 Kings 7 how the Lord's words allowed the lord to see the blessing but never to walk in it, never to enjoy it, but only to see it from afar.

I am sure we all agree that we do not want our husbands to speak a word from God but we doubt the promise and speak against it. We do not want the consequence of only our husbands enjoying the promise manifested. No, ladies, I don't think any of us want to be on the outside looking in. So pray when you do not understand, and be careful of giving an evil report.

Now let's look at another Old Testament example. God will sometimes give us just what we say, so we must be careful of each word we speak. God even hears when we laugh within ourselves as Sarah did. Let's read the record in Genesis 18:9–15:

And they said unto him, Where is Sarah thy wife? And he said, Behold, in the tent. And he said, I will certainly return unto thee according to the time of life; and, lo, Sarah thy wife shall have a son. And Sarah heard it in the tent door, which was behind him. Now Abraham and Sarah were old and well stricken in age; and it ceased to be with Sarah after the manner of women. Therefore Sarah laughed within herself, saying, After I am waxed old shall I have pleasure, my lord being old also? And the LORD said unto Abraham, Wherefore did Sarah laugh, saying, Shall I of a surety bear a child, which am old? Is any thing too hard for the LORD? At the time appointed I will return unto thee, according to the time of life, and Sarah shall have a son. Then Sarah denied, saying, I laughed not; for she was afraid. And he said, Nay; but thou didst laugh.

The funny thing about this Scripture that stands out in my mind is that God questioned Abraham when He heard Sarah laughed. Is your husband having to pray or answer for your doubt, for your laughter, for your unbelief?

I think we need to pause and ask why Sarah laughed. You see, something was going on within her. Could it be that our sister Sarah could not believe the promise given to her husband because she had so much fear and low self-esteem that she really could not believe for herself? You see, sometimes life can be so harsh that we begin to believe we deserve what has happened to us, that we do not deserve to have anything better. Or we develop a defense mechanism that immediately jokes about something so we won't believe for it and therefore won't be disappointed and thus won't be hurt. And these small concessions turn out to be large roadblocks in our lives and our family's lives. You see, Sarah could not believe the promise for Abraham because she could not see it for herself.

Ladies, we need to deal with our feelings of fear, doubt, and disbelief first. You see, if we stop and really search ourselves, we will find that these feelings are tied to previous experiences in our lives that may have disappointed or hurt us. As a result, we have built a defense mechanism where we laugh within ourselves. Now I use the phrase laugh within ourselves here, but really you have to answer for yourself, what is it that you do? You must deal with these feelings here and now, even if you need to stop reading. Do some journaling perhaps, but you need to kill this spirit of doubt that causes you to speak even small words of doubt. Sarah even later denied her laughter. You see, you must trust God's Word for just what it says.

Okay, maybe we need to go another way. What if it's not you, but, being honest, your husband is the one who has disappointed you? He has broken promises. He has made mistakes that negatively impacted you and your family. Well, let's just say it. He has hurt you. You are not healed from the wounds, and your small words are coming from a place of pain. Now we are not saying that you don't love him. But you don't want to be disappointed or hurt again, so you give a quick answer, never really hearing him or praying for his next career move, invention, move in ministry, whatever it is. You just laugh. This is your defense so that he does not hurt you again. But laughing and being defensive is not the answer.

This, too, ladies, is a trick of the enemy! See, we have to stop and pray for ourselves first: God, search me. Have I been hurt in the past to the point I can't dream for myself or even encourage someone else? Help me, God. Have I embraced a spirit of disappointment, pain, and offense? Have I allowed them to take residence in my life to the point that I operate under these spirits? God, I pray You heal me now! Touch me supernaturally, God. In every place in my life that has been bruised, heal me. Help me to dream again. Help me to believe again. Help me to encourage and motivate others to dream also.

Remember that the children of Israel received just what they spoke as they complained. The shortest phrase can make all the difference; words like "yes, Lord" can be powerful and change the course of lives, impacting generations. So I pray each of us will be careful of the small things. I know we are not perfect. The tongue is the hardest thing to tame, but as Proverbs 21:23 says, "Whoso keepeth his mouth and his tongue keepeth his soul from troubles."

With God's help, you can build your home with the smallest things, with simple words like "yes, Lord" and "God's will be done," or "by the grace of God" and "God said it." These words will first change you. These words will change your outlook on any situation, thereby changing your attitude from a negative to a positive one.

You see, as you begin speaking life-giving words pertaining to God's Word, you are changing the atmosphere. Once you have a different perspective, then it is easy to encourage your husband and build him up with words like "I believe in you," "I will stand with you and wait on God," or "I'm with you, baby." Always include yourself in the support of your husband with questions like "What do you want us to do?" and "Where should we go from here?" Always let him know as you go together that you support him. Sometimes the small things, the small words, make all the difference.

Chapter 10

Even the Small Things Matter

Chapter Prayer

God, help me to see that even the small things
matter.
Every word that is spoken with my tongue is either
giving life or death.
God, help me to always recognize when my words
are not giving life.

God, as I read Your Word daily,
wash and renew my mind.
I want to be the kind of woman who builds and does
not tear down.

I pray my words are words of encouragement
and not discouragement,
words that lift up!
Every word I speak matters and will bring life.

God, help me to speak only life
every phrase, every sentence, even words under my
breath.
Help me to speak according to Your will.

I pray all that I say will bring glory to You, God.

In the name of Jesus,
Amen.

Chapter 11

Give the Enemy No Place
☙⫷

Ephesians 4:27: "Neither give place to the devil."

From the beginning of time, the enemy has been trying to find a way in, a way to destroy the creation of God. The devil is jealous and upset with the relationship man has with God, and he is always seeking to discredit and destroy man. He started looking for a place in through conversation with Eve in the garden of Eden, a place in by using crafty words. And just like he did with Eve, the first wife, he is still looking for a place in through the wife today. The devil knows that the wife has a tender place in her husband's heart, so if he can get the wife, he can get the husband.

Let me go further in my explanation. God has been shifting the church into kingdom order. As we can see, the body of Christ has been changing to incorporate both the husband and the wife into leadership. God is taking us back to Genesis 1:26: *"And God said, Let us make man in our image, after our likeness: and let them have dominion"*. We are beginning to see husbands and wives laboring in ministry, pastoring, and preaching together like never before. Husbands and wives are beginning to team together, and the result is well-balanced, God ordained ministries that move forcefully in the will of God and destroy the kingdom of darkness by leaps and bounds. The enemy sees this and hates what God is doing, because a husband and wife who work together exemplify the word of God that says, *"This is now bone of my bones, and flesh of my flesh: she shall be called Woman, because she was taken out of Man"* (Gen. 2:23).

Now, instead of one man having two lives, one at home and one at church, he and his wife have one life together. The enemy now sees the wife, the second person, which makes two in agreement, operating with her husband, and he knows he has two pastoring together instead of one. And when they agree with the same mind, then the Scriptures come to life in their ministry. As Matthew 18:19 says, "Again I say unto you, That if two of you shall agree on earth as touching any thing that they shall ask, it shall be done for them of my Father which is in heaven." There is only victory for the husband and wife in agreement. The enemy hates this, so he looks for a place to come in and destroy the unity.

Look at what the Bible says can happen when we agree. Genesis 11:6 says, *"And the LORD said, Behold, the people is one, and they have all one language; and this they begin to do: and now nothing will be restrained from them, which they have imagined to do"* .

God's Word further states the importance of two operating together to help each other to labor to restore, to comfort each other, and to prevail against anyone who comes against the two. Ecclesiastes 4:9–12 reads: *"Two are better than one; because they have a good reward for their labour.*

For if they fall, the one will lift up his fellow: but woe to him that is alone when he falleth; for he hath not another to help him up. Again, if two lie together, then they have heat: but how can one be warm alone? And if one prevail against him, two shall withstand him; and a threefold cord is not quickly broken."

Together we outnumber the enemy with the strength of unity. There is an anointing on our unity. Leviticus 26:8 says, *"And five of you shall chase an hundred, and an hundred of you shall put ten thousand to flight: and your enemies shall fall before you by the sword"*; and Deuteronomy says in 32:30, *"How should one chase a thousand, and two put ten thousand to flight, except their Rock had sold them, and the LORD had shut them up?"*

The enemy knows he can't effectively fight the two of you together unified, so he tries to find a place in, a wedge to distract. But he won't do it—in the name of Jesus! Be encouraged, for God's Word tells us what to do. Look at these Scriptures that give us keys to keep the enemy away. We will not be deceived by his old tricks.

Ephesians 4:27 says, *"Neither give place to the devil"*; and Ephesians 6:11 continues with, *"Put on the whole armour of God, that ye may be able to stand against the wiles of the devil."* Let's not forget James 4:7 *"Submit yourselves therefore to God. Resist the devil, and he will flee from you."* And God tells us to always be aware of who the enemy is in 1 Peter 5:8: *"Be sober, be vigilant; because your adversary the devil, as a roaring lion, walketh about, seeking whom he may devour."* You see, God assures us of the victory when we follow His Word.

I am sure you could name countless examples of women you know or knew who have been attacked with such a veracity you knew the attack was purposed to distract and cause her family to lose focus. Let's expose the enemy so he can never do this to another sister.

In this chapter, we are going to expose the enemy for the deceiver he is, how he tries to distract us and our husbands. How does he do this? In this chapter, we are going to discuss two forms of attack. There are other avenues of attack, but we are going to concentrate on only these two in this chapter. The first way he comes in is through whispering subtle lies, and the second is through attacking our bodies. You see, in both cases he causes the husband and family to become distracted, off focus, because of their concern for their wife and mother.

Door number one is the lie. You see, Satan's weapons are really old. The lies are the oldest. He talks through family members and through friends, all to get you off balance. Once he has you hooked on a lie, then he brings in doubt and often fear. The next thing you know, here comes isolation. And then you find yourself doubtful, depressed, discouraged, and alone.

Or the enemy may try to use the wife by telling her lies, hoping she will pass them on to her husband. Just like he did with Eve, he whispers crafty lies to the woman in an attempt to get her off balance. Don't let lies cause you to doubt yourself, no matter the source. The enemy will use whomever he can.

Door number two is the body. We must guard our bodies against sickness and disease. If we are sick, it will render us unable to work effectively in ministry. In some cases, the enemy is actually trying to take our very lives. But he is a liar, because no weapon formed against us will prosper. I encourage each of you to fight for your body's health.

What do I mean? Not only should we women proclaim we are healthy and whole, but we should be proactive in our wellness. We cannot abuse our bodies, pushing them continually without rest. As women, we do not always take care of ourselves; we are often the last to be cared for. But we must learn how to care for ourselves and care for ourselves well. I don't mean in a selfish manner, but knowing our bodies are the temple of the Lord, we should care for them.

How do we do this? We don't just eat anything. We eat what will be good for our bodies. We go to the doctor regularly. We watch levels like cholesterol, blood sugar, and iron. We have mammograms when appropriate. We put works with our faith. We proclaim the enemy shall not use our bodies against our husbands' and families' purposes.

I bet you never thought about it that way. A husband who cares for his wife, his good thing, can't concentrate as sharply if he is concerned for his wife. But we do not have to be doors for the enemy to distract us or our husbands.

Many of us can testify of great attacks that come to divide our marriages, and often the attacks come right before God is about to give increase in an aspect of our lives. We should recognize whom the attack is coming from and seek God for the answer. Do not panic or blame your husband during this time, but come together with him. It does not matter who did what for the purpose of blame. We should want to know who did what only so we can learn from the experience and learn what to do differently next time.

Even as our children grow, they will make mistakes, sometimes even falling or seeming to go backwards, but this too is a part of growing. As children of God, we may have setbacks, but we do not have to let setbacks set our marriages back. Don't throw your marriage away because the two people in it made a mistake! Look at everything you are going through as an opportunity to work together, learning something else about each other and appreciating each other. Do not blame each other for where you are; instead, know that God has the plans for your life. Trust Him, and rest in the peace of God. Stand in agreement with your husband. Stand together and walk so closely that you give the enemy no doorway in, no way to cause confusion, hurt, or strife. Give the enemy no place.

Chapter 11

Give the Enemy No Place

Chapter Prayer

Sovereign God!
Omnipotent God!
I thank You for my life partner.
I thank You, God, for showing me that we are
strong together.
I bless You, God, for showing me through Your
Word that there is order in unity,
that if we stand together in Your Word to
accomplish Your will,
nothing can be withheld from us!

Now God, I pray You expose every lying tongue
and every deceitful whisper that would try to invade
my marriage.
I bind the spirit of division that the enemy would
use to move into my marriage.
And God, if there are places where my husband and
I have let the enemy in,
I first pray for Your forgiveness
and I pray Lord show us where and through who
the enemie may have entered into our relationship.

Teach me, God, by Your Holy Spirit,
how to see the enemy when he comes
and how to keep doors closed that the enemy would
seek to come through.
I pray for sharpened discernment to see and to know
and to spoil the attack of the enemy.

God, I pray for my marriage now, that it will be
stronger from this moment on.

In Jesus' name,
Amen.

Chapter 12

God, the Ultimate Rewarder

৩\৫

W e have talked so much of preparing ourselves, of understanding that we are suitable and chosen, and of the what, how, and when to give. But I want to make sure we discuss what the helpmeet receives, because I would be wrong if I did not encourage you to learn to be a receiver also. I want to encourage each of you that God is your ultimate rewarder. In all you do, you should do it as unto the Lord; all you do will be for His glory.

However, sometimes when we help someone through words, deeds, or prayers, we, in our flesh, expect some kind of reciprocating act from the individual we have helped. But often our rewards are not given in the same way or from the same person. God's principle of reaping and sowing does tell us of our reaping, but it does not guarantee the source will be the same.

Galatians 6:7–9 reads, *"Do not be deceived, God is not mocked; for whatever a man sows, that he will also reap. For he that sows to his flesh will of the flesh reap corruption, but he who sows to the Spirit will of the Spirit reap everlasting life. And let us not grow weary while doing good for in due season we shall reap if we do not lose heart"* (NKJV). In Matthew 6:3–4, the Word also says God will reward us openly: *"But when thou doest alms, let not thy left hand know what thy right hand doeth: That thine alms may be in secret: and thy Father which seeth in secret himself shall reward thee openly."* So in all your helping, faint not!

Let's look at an illustration of God being the ultimate provider. I would like to look at a text in 2 Kings in particular, because in the past whenever I would read this, I would become irritated for some reason. But God has changed my point of view. Let's look at the prophet's wife in 2 Kings 4:1–7:

> *"Now there cried a certain woman of the wives of the sons of the prophets unto Elisha, saying, Thy servant my husband is dead; and thou knowest that thy servant did fear the LORD: and the creditor is come to take unto him my two sons to be bondmen. And Elisha said unto her, What shall I do for thee? tell me, what hast thou in the house? And she said, Thine handmaid hath not any thing in the house, save a pot of oil. Then he said, Go, borrow thee vessels abroad of all thy neighbours, even empty vessels; borrow not a few. And when thou art come in, thou shalt shut the door upon thee and upon thy sons, and shalt pour out into all those vessels, and thou shalt set aside that which is full. So she went from him, and shut the door upon her and upon her sons, who brought the vessels to her; and she poured out. And it came to pass, when the vessels were full, that she said unto her son, Bring me yet a vessel. And he said unto her, There is not a vessel more. And the oil stayed. Then she came and told the man of God. And he said, Go, sell the oil, and pay thy debt, and live thou and thy children of the rest."*

When I first read 2 Kings 4, my main emphasis was on the fact that this woman's husband was a prophet who feared the Lord and was a servant of Elisha or one of his students in the school of the prophets. How could this man of God die and leave his wife without properly providing for her or without leaving an inheritance for his sons? How could a man who feared the Lord have not provided for his family? I don't know; maybe I was internalizing the Scriptures because I am married and have children. I would not want this to happen to me. So I just stopped reading, never getting the full understanding. But God has plans for me and you, just like He did for the prophet's wife.

Time, really years passed from when I first read this Scripture. My family was in a season where God was showing Himself as a provider, the ultimate provider. Remember, God is always our ultimate source. He may use our husbands as a resource, but God is the source. During this season, God brought me back to the prophet's wife in 2 Kings 4 and began talking to me concerning the prophet's wife. God ministered to me that He is the source of all we need. He reassured me that although He may work through our husbands as provider, He will ultimately give us all we need.

As I read through the verses, I found one great quality about the wife. She did know enough to go to the man of God. During that time, the prophet of God was the voice of God; his words were the words of God. He was God's way of giving people guidance. So we can say she went to the "Word of God" for her answer.

This is a great example for us today, especially when the people in our lives that we thought would be a source of help don't help us. It can sometimes be a disappointment when our loved ones, spouses, parents, children, and friends are not able to or just don't help us. Sometimes this can cause us to have hurt feelings and blame others. But the truth is, God often has us in a place where only He can help us. He wants to show us that He alone is our provider.

Returning to the widow, she received direction in verses 3 and 4 from the voice of God, His word. She went and did all he said, and she followed the direction of God through Elisha. God was providing for her even after her husband died. So here we see that though one resource may end, God will always find a way to bless you.

This text does not talk about the woman's relationship with her husband, nor does it talk about her faithfulness or obedience to God. It does not say she was a perfect wife. It only calls her a wife. Ha! That's us! Therefore, we can only speculate what had happened here. I think God added the fact that she was married and married to a man of God for our benefit. It speaks to all wives who read it. It merely speaks that God will provide for us.

Elisha's last recorded direction to this woman was, "Pay thy debt, and live thou and thy children of the rest." God so rewarded her until her abundance was so great that she could pay all her debt and take care of herself and her children. There was more than enough. This woman lost nothing. There was no lack; instead, there was abundance for herself and her children. The threat against her sons was void.

The blessing for me in this text is that God has His ladies in mind, and He is showing us that He is more than able to take care of us. That's why His Word tells us to cast all our cares *"and to be careful for nothing"* (Phil. 4:6).

Sometimes we may get concerned about where God has us in a particular season in our lives. The enemy tries to make us open to the spirit of fear. The enemy whispers things like, "If he answers his call to ministry, you are going to be broke"; " If he sows this seed, you will not be able to pay the rent"; "If he works in the church on the weekend, he will have to stop working that part-time job, and you will never get the down payment for the house"; "If he is spending so much time at the church, when will he spend time with you?"; "What about the children? Who will care for them, feed them, nurture them?"

The enemy will try to taunt us with all that we will lose by use of the word *if*. If he succeeds, we will begin to live contrary to Philippians 4:6, and we will try to manipulate and control our husbands into staying home with us.

Now I had better stop here and make sure we are all together. I am one who believes the Scriptures, so I believe Timothy 5:8: *"But if any provide not for his own, and specially for those of his own house, he hath denied the faith, and is worse than an infidel."* I do believe all ministers of the gospel should minister at home first. But let's continue; we were talking about the deceptive ifs of the enemy. I have one more if, maybe the biggest if: "What will happen if I sow greatly into my husband? If I help him, who will care for me? Who will love me?"

Whether you choose to admit it, I know I am telling the truth. You see, until we totally trust God, we will always have these questions about our needs being met. The enemy seeks to trap us in fear, and then all our direction turns toward ourselves instead of toward what God wants for us. We begin always asking questions like the following: "What about me?" "What about my dreams?" "What about my desires?" "What about my goals?" "Who is going to be for me?" But this is a trap to cause us to be in so much fear that we stop or nag our husbands until they stop!

But I have a greater if. What if our husbands listen to us? What if they hearken to our voices and we are wrong? We already talked about this in chapter 6. You see, that's why it is so important to know God for ourselves. If we know He is our provider and healer, we won't become overly concerned or jealous of our husbands' time with God or in ministry, because we will understand our husbands have a purpose and a calling, just as we do. God is looking for willing and obedient children that He can bless.

Let's look at what the Scriptures say about God caring for us. The answer is spelled out clearly in the Word of God. 1 Peter 5:7 says, *"Casting all your care upon him; for he careth for you"*; and Psalm 55:22 says, *"Cast thy burden upon the LORD, and he shall sustain thee: he shall never suffer the righteous to be moved."*

Furthermore, Matthew 6:25 says, *"Therefore I say unto you, Take no thought for your life, what ye shall eat, or what ye shall drink; nor yet for your body, what ye shall put on. Is not the life more than meat, and the body than raiment?"* Philippians 4:6 reads, *"Be careful for nothing; but in every thing by prayer and supplication with thanksgiving let your requests be made known unto God."*

Hebrews 13:5 instructs, *"Let your conversation be without covetousness; and be content with such things as ye have: for he hath said, I will never leave thee, nor forsake thee."* And Psalm 34:15 promises, *"The eyes of the LORD are upon the righteous, and his ears are open unto their cry."*

Psalm 34:17 assures us, *"The righteous cry, and the LORD heareth, and delivereth them out of all their troubles."* Isaiah 41:10 declares, *"Fear thou not; for I am with thee: be not dismayed; for I am thy God: I will strengthen thee; yea, I will help thee; yea, I will uphold thee with the right hand of my righteousness."*

I have another illustration: let's look at Abraham. To tell the truth, I was a little upset with the father of faith, the friend of God, Abraham. A couple of times, I felt he placed his wife, his jewel, his gift from God, in an awkward situation by acting like she was not his wife. He told men that might look upon her and find her beautiful that she was his sister, out of fear of what they would do to him. Let's look at the two Scriptures. The first incident is recorded in Genesis

12:10–20, and the second incident is recorded in Genesis 20:1–18.

Just think about it. Sarai was Abram's wife. She was obedient to her husband when he said, "We are moving away from this land, from all your family, from everything that is familiar and has made you comfortable. I want you to go with me, and on top of all of this, I will tell you where we are going when I know." Sarai believed her husband and journeyed forward with him.

But when they got into a foreign land, this man, her husband, began acting like she was not the good thing God had given him. What! Sarai had to be questioning some things. She must have thought, Haven't I been with you? Why, my husband, do you treat me this way, and not once, but twice! You see, he was ready to give her over to other men twice. What worse thing could a husband do to his wife? I don't want to get into the reasons for Abram's acts as much as the effect this must have had on Sarai. I am sure she did not want her husband to be hurt or to fall into harm, so she went along with the deception. But was he prepared to leave her with these men? Maybe she wondered about the fulfillment of God's promises concerning her future.

But stay encouraged, because I told you God has our backs. In the text, it says in Genesis 12:11–17:

> *"As he was about to enter Egypt, he said to his wife Sarai, "I know what a beautiful woman you are. When the Egyptians see you, they will say, 'This is his wife.' Then they will kill me but will let you live. Say you are my sister, so that I will be treated well for your sake and my life will be spared because of you. When Abram came to Egypt, the Egyptians saw that she was a very beautiful woman. And when Pharaoh's officials saw her, they praised her to Pharaoh, and she was taken into his palace. He treated Abram well*

for her sake, and Abram acquired sheep and cattle, male and female donkeys, menservants and maid-servants, and camels. But the Lord inflicted serious diseases on Pharaoh and his household because of Abram's wife Sarai. So Pharaoh summoned Abram. "What have you done to me?" he said. "Why didn't you tell me she was your wife? Why did you say, 'She is my sister,' so that I took her to be my wife? Now then, here is your wife. Take her and go!" Then Pharaoh gave orders about Abram to his men, and they sent him on his way, with his wife and every-thing he had. (NIV)"

The second time is recorded in Genesis 20:1–18:

And Abraham journeyed from thence toward the south country, and dwelled between Kadesh and Shur, and sojourned in Gerar. And Abraham said of Sarah his wife, She is my sister: and Abimelech king of Gerar sent, and took Sarah.

But God came to Abimelech in a dream by night, and said to him, Behold, thou art but a dead man, for the woman which thou hast taken; for she is a man's wife. But Abimelech had not come near her: and he said, Lord, wilt thou slay also a righteous nation? Said he not unto me, She is my sister? and she, even she herself said, He is my brother: in the integrity of my heart and innocency of my hands have I done this. And God said unto him in a dream, Yea, I know that thou didst this in the integrity of thy heart; for I also withheld thee from sinning against me: there-fore suffered I thee not to touch her. Now therefore restore the man his wife; for he is a prophet, and he shall pray for thee, and thou shalt live: and if thou restore her not, know thou that thou shalt surely die, thou, and all that are thine.

Therefore Abimelech rose early in the morning, and called all his servants, and told all these things in their ears: and the men were sore afraid. Then Abimelech called Abraham, and said unto him, What hast thou done unto us? and what have I offended thee, that thou hast brought on me and on my kingdom a great sin? thou hast done deeds unto me that ought not to be done. And Abimelech said unto Abraham, What sawest thou, that thou hast done this thing? And Abraham said, Because I thought, Surely the fear of God is not in this place; and they will slay me for my wife's sake. And yet indeed she is my sister; she is the daughter of my father, but not the daughter of my mother; and she became my wife. And it came to pass, when God caused me to wander from my father's house, that I said unto her, This is thy kindness which thou shalt show unto me; at every place whither we shall come, say of me, He is my brother.

And Abimelech took sheep, and oxen, and menservants, and women servants, and gave them unto Abraham, and restored him Sarah his wife. And Abimelech said, Behold, my land is before thee: dwell where it pleaseth thee. And unto Sarah he said, Behold, I have given thy brother a thousand pieces of silver: behold, he is to thee a covering of the eyes, unto all that are with thee, and with all other: thus she was reproved. So Abraham prayed unto God: and God healed Abimelech, and his wife, and his maidservants; and they bare children. For the LORD had fast closed up all the wombs of the house of Abimelech, because of Sarah Abraham's wife.

Then, after this, it happened again, but this time with Isaac, Abraham's son! But don't worry; God was still in charge.

Genesis 26:7–11 records:

And the men of the place asked him of his wife; and he said, She is my sister: for he feared to say, She is my wife; lest, said he, the men of the place should kill me for Rebekah; because she was fair to look upon. And it came to pass, when he had been there a long time, that Abimelech king of the Philistines looked out at a window, and saw, and, behold, Isaac was sporting with Rebekah his wife. And Abimelech called Isaac, and said, Behold, of a surety she is thy wife: and how saidst thou, She is my sister? And Isaac said unto him, Because I said, Lest I die for her. And Abimelech said, What is this thou hast done unto us? one of the people might lightly have lien with thy wife, and thou shouldest have brought guiltiness upon us. And Abimelech charged all his people, saying, He that toucheth this man or his wife shall surely be put to death.

In all these examples, the wife must have felt left behind and betrayed. I want to give assurance to women here. In each example, God did surely bring each wife out and with no harm. This is a great place to stop and point out God's faithfulness to the wife. God showed up in each example to demonstrate His faithfulness toward her. Even when the people we expect to stand up for us can't or won't, God will always be our champion. Remember God is your rewarder.

Chapter 12

God, the Ultimate Rewarder

Chapter Prayer

God, please forgive me for ever doubting that You
were a sovereign God.
Forgive me for letting the spirit of fear put me into
bondage,
causing me to not give all that You told me to give.

God, help me to trust You for everything!
Help me not to serve you with closed hands,
grasping for what I need, but with open hands to
receive from You.
Teach me, Lord, to give as You direct
and to look to You for the reaping of my harvest.

God, I also want to forgive all those I have held
in debt
as if they owe me something.
Forgive me for being upset with people because
they did not or could not help me.

God, I want all I do to please You.
I look to You for all I need.
God, You are my ultimate provider.

In the name of Jesus,
Amen.

Chapter 13

The Last Good Word
❧❧

The Benediction

After all has been said and done, make sure you cast all your cares on the Lord, for He cares for you. Ha! That is the essence of this book. God is going to do it, but "not by might, nor by power . . ."

When we started this journey, we began with preparing, nurturing, and maturing our relationship with God through our Lord Jesus Christ, caring for our inner man so we could become, go, and do. Then we discussed God's purpose in our making. We moved to interaction and communication with our husbands and discussed how to be a nurturer, supporter, and encourager God's way. And last we hit on the true source, God.

I pray you ladies see that we have made a full circle and come back to where we started: to God and our relationship with him. Hopefully you have come to realize that in all things we need Christ. So trust God.

The last illustration I want to leave with you has to deal with the Waterford vase we talked about in the first chapter, "Help Yourself First!" We said that the Waterford vase was created for a purpose, beautifully and wonderfully made, and it was of great value to the creator. The creator wanted it to fulfill its purpose, to be a great serving vessel used to pour into and out of. We said to let God pour into you so you can pour out to others, because until you are poured into, you cannot pour out. Without the pouring in, you will never be used. Now as we come to the end of our journey in this book, I want to add some additional Scripture on pouring in and pouring out for you to meditate on.

John 4:14: *"But whosoever drinketh of the water that I shall give him shall never thirst; but the water that I shall give him shall be in him a well of water springing up into everlasting life."*

Proverbs 11:24: *"There is that scattereth, and yet increaseth; and there is that withholdeth more than is meet, but it tendeth to poverty."*

Proverbs 11:25: *"The liberal soul shall be made fat: and he that watereth shall be watered also himself."*

Proverbs 11:26: *"He that withholdeth corn, the people shall curse him: but blessing shall be upon the head of him that selleth it."*

As you read the Scriptures, focus on God, your provider, comforter, and counselor. Everything you need comes from God. Remember, He is going to pour into you; He will give you everything you need.

The knowledge of God as your answer causes you to be centered, grounded, and focused on God. The small, troublesome matters or even the large details of the day become smaller as you focus on God. Your focus turns from the problem to the God who has the answer. Then you are able to rest in God's ability to handle whatever you are going through. This is the most liberating revelation we as women must grasp.

As women, sometimes we are used to handling all the details in order to work to the bigger picture, but God wants all our cares. He does not want us burdened. Matthew 11:28–

30 says, *"Come unto me, all ye that labour and are heavy laden, and I will give you rest. Take my yoke upon you, and learn of me; for I am meek and lowly in heart: and ye shall find rest unto your souls. For my yoke is easy, and my burden is light."* We must yield all control to Him so He can use us. We need to be free of burdensome problems so we can serve God and He can work through us.

God cares so much for us that He even wants to prepare us for what is coming. There could be a crisis in someone else's life, and God wants to use us to give a word of encouragement. But if we have not spent time with Him, we will not be prepared and the other person will not be helped. Consistent time with God will make all the difference in our lives.

As women, we are often responsible for setting the atmosphere of our homes. In other words, we set the tone of the home. However, if we are tired, haggard, or stressed, the home will probably show itself with disorganization, confusion, clutter, tension, and stress. It is important that we first let God through His Word and the assistance of His Spirit help us. We must remember that in all things He is our ultimate source. His Word says He will give us all we need.

I want to leave you with this Scripture, Proverbs 11:25, because it completes our journey with the understanding that as we help, God helps, and as we give, God gives. Don't worry about giving all you have. Don't concern yourself with pouring yourself out. Remember, *"He that watereth shall be watered also himself."* One thing God has done for me is that He has sent me encouragement when I encouraged others. He sent me help as I helped. You cannot do more for others than God can do for you.

Chapter 13

The Last Good Word

Chapter Prayer

God, thank You for my journey.

Lord, I pray that I will continue to grow as a wife.
I pray You will continue to teach me with Your
Word and Your Holy Spirit
so that I may please You.
God, I pray that my marriage will glorify You and
Your purpose.

God, I will put my relationship with You first
so that You can first tell me who I am and what I am
to do,
so that You will feed me and build me.
Then, God, teach me who, when, and how to help.
For every life I touch, I pray my words and deeds
point back to You.

In the name of Jesus,
Amen.

LaVergne, TN USA
25 January 2011
213927LV00001B/36/P